The Holy Koran of the Moorish

Divinely Prepared by the Noble Prophet
DREW ALI

Reprint of the Original 1926 Publication

Courtesy of Bro. Tallahassee Bey
&
Grand Sheik, Bro. Kudjo Adwo El
M.S.T. of A. # 5 Canaanland—Toronto

Prepared for Publication by
Sis. Tauheedah S. Najee-Ullah El

© 2014

Califa Media™
A Moorish Guide Publishing
Company
califamedia@gmail.com

All Rights, Remedies, and Liberties Reserved

Know Thyself and Allah.

THE GENEOLOGY OF "JESUS"

Life and Works of Jesus in India, Europe and Africa, in the land of Egypt.

NOBLE DREW ALI

THE PROPHET AND FOUNDER OF THE MOORISH HOLY
TEMPLE OF SCIENCE, TO REDEEM THE PEOPLE
FROM THEIR SINFUL WAYS.

SULTAN ABDUL AZIZ IBU SUAD

THE DESCENDANT OF HAGAR, NOW THE HEAD OF THE
HOLY CITY OF MECCA.

KNOW THYSELF
AND THY FATHER GOD.
ALLAH.

The Geneology of Jesus with eighteen years of the events, life, works and teachings in India, Europe and Africa. These events occurred before He was thirty years of age. These secret lessons are for all of those who love Jesus and desire to know about His life works and teachings.

Dear readers, do not falsely use these lessons. They are for good, peace and happiness for all those that love Jesus.

Dear mothers, teach these lessons to your little ones, that they may learn to love instead of hate.

Dear fathers, by these lessons you can set your house in order and your children will learn to love instead of to hate.

The lessons of this pamphlet are not for sale, but for the sake of humanity, as I am a prophet and the servant is worthy of his hire, you can receive this pamphlet at expense. The reason these lessons have not been known is because the Moslems of India, Egypt and Palestine had these secrets and kept them back from the outside world, and when the time appointed by Allah they loosen the keys and freed these secrets, and for the first time in ages have these secrets been delivered in the hands of the Moslems of America. All authority and rights of publishing of this pamphlet of 1927

By the Prophet

NOBLE DREW ALI

The industrious acts of the Moslems of northwest and southwest Africa. These are the Moabites, Hamathites, Canaanites, who were driven out of the land of Canaan, by Joshua, and received permission from the Pharoahs of Egypt to settle in that portion of Egypt. In later years they formed themselves kingdoms. These kingdoms are called this day Morocco, Algiers, Tunis, Tripoli, etc.

CHAPTER I.

THE CREATION AND FALL OF MAN

"Time never was, when man was not." If life of man at any time began, a time would come when it would end. "The thoughts of Allah cannot be circumscribed. No finite mind can comprehend things infinite." All finite things are subject unto change. All finite things will cease to be because there was a time when they were not." The bodies and the souls of men are finite things, and they will change, yea, from the finite point of view the time will come when they will be no more. "But man himself is not the body, nor the soul; he is a spirit and a part of Allah." Creative Fate gave to man, to spirit-man, a soul that he might function on the plane of soul; gave him a body of flesh, that he might function on the plane of things made manifest. "Why did Creative Fate give to spirit-man a soul that he might function on the plane of soul? Why did Creative Fate give to soul a body of flesh that he might function on the plane of things that are made manifest? Hear, now, ye cherubim, ye seraphim, ye angels and ye men!

"Hear, now, oh protoplast and earth and plant and beast!

"Hear, now, ye creeping things of earth, ye fish that swim, ye birds that fly!

Hear, now, ye winds that blow, ye thunders and ye lightnings of the sky.

"Hear, now, ye spirits of the fire, of water, earth and air.

"Hear, now, oh everything that is, or was, or ever more will be, for wisdom speaks from out the highest plane of spirit life:

"Man is a thought of Allah; all things of Allah are infinite; they are not measured up by time, for the things that are concerned with time, begin and end.

"The thoughts of Allah, are the everlasting of the past unto the never ending days to come. And so is man, the spirit-man.

"But man like every other thought of Allah, was but a seed, a seed that held within itself the potencies of Allah, just as the seed of any plant of earth holds deep within itself the attributes of every part of that especial plant.

"So spirit-man as seed of Allah held deep within himself the attributes of every part of Allah.

"Now, seeds are perfect, yea, as perfect as the source from which they come; but they are not unfolded into life made manifest. The child is as perfect as the mother is. So man, the seed must be deeply planted in a soil that he might grow, unfold, as does the bud unfold to show the flower. The human seed that came forth from the heart of Allah was full ordained to be the Lord of the plane of soul, and of the plane of things made manifest. So Allah, the husbandman of everything that is, threw forth this human seed into the soil of soul; it grew apace, and man became a living soul, and he became the Lord of all the kingdom of the soul. Hark, now, let every creature hear; the plane of the soul is but the ether of the spirit plane vibrating not so fast, and in the slower rhythm of this plane the essence of life are manifest; the perfumes and the odors, the true sensations and the all of love manifest.

"And these soul attributes became a body beautiful. A multitude of lessons man must learn upon the plane of soul; and here he tarries many ages untitl his lessons are all learned. Upon the boundary of the plane of soul; there he must overcome, yea, overcome them every one. essences took on a final garb; the perfumes and odors and the true sensations and the all of love were clothed in flesh; and man was clothed in flesh. Perfected man must pass through all the ways of life, and so a carnel was full manifest, a nature that sprang forth from fleshy things. Without a foe a soldier never knows his strength, and thought must be developed by the exercise of strength. And so this carnal nature soon became a foe that man must fight, that he might be the strength of Allah made manifest. Let every living thing stand still and hear! Man is the Lord of all the plane of manifest, or protoplast, of mineral, of plant, of beast; but he given up his birthrights just to gratify his lower self. But man will regain his lost estate, his heritage; but he must do it in a conflict that cannot be told in words. Yet he must suffer trials and temptations manifold; but let him know that cheribum and seraphim that rule the stations of the sun and spirit of the mighty Allah who rule the solar stars are his protectors and his guide and they will lead to victory. Man will be fully saved, redeemed, perfected by the things he suffers on the plane of flesh, and on the plane of soul. When man has conquered carnal things his garb of flesh will then have served its purpose well and it will fall; will be no more.

"Then he will stand untrammeled on the plane of soul where he must full complete his victories. Unnumbered foes will stand before man upon the plane of soul; there he must overcome, yea, overcome them every one. Thus hope will ever be his beacon light; there is no failure for the human soul, for Allah is leading on and victory is sure.

"Man cannot die; the spirit man is one with Allah, and while Allah lives man cannot die. When man has conquered every foe upon the plane of soul the seed will have full opened out, will have unfolded in the Holy Breath. The garb of soul will then have served its purpose well, and man will need it never more, and it will pass and be no more and man will then attain unto the blessedness of perfectness and at one with Allah."

CHAPTER II.

EDUCATION OF MARY AND ELIZABETH IN ZOAN, EGYPT

1. The son of Herod, Archelaus, reigned in Jerusalem. He was a selfish, cruel king; he put to death all those who did not honor him.

2. He called in council all the wisest men and asked the infant claimant of his throne.

3. The council said that John and Jesus both were dead; then he was satisfied.

4. Now Joseph, Mary and their son were in Egypt in Zoan, and John was with his mother in the Judean hills.

5. Elihu and Salome sent messengers in haste to find Elizabeth and John. They found them, they brought them to Zoan.

6. Now Mary and Elizabeth were marveling much because of their deliverance.

7. Elihu said, "It is not strange; there are no happenings; law governs all events."

8. From olden times it was ordained that you should be with us and in this sacred school be taught.

9. Elihu and Salome took Mary and Elizabeth out to the sacred grove nearby where they were wont to teach.

10. Elihu said to Mary and Elizabeth, you may esteem yourselves thrice blessed, for you are chosen mothers of long promised sons.

11. Who are ordained to lay a solid rock a sure foundation stone on which the temple of the perfect man shall rest—a temple that shall never be destroyed.

12. We measure time by cycle ages, and the gate to every age we deem a mile stone in the journey of the race.

13. An age had passed; the gate unto another age flies open at the age touch of time. This is the preparation age of soul, the kingdom of Immanuel, of Allah in man.

14. And, these, your sons, will be the first to tell the news, and teach the gospel of good will to men, and peace on earth.

15. A mighty work is theirs, for carnal men want not the light; they love the dark, and when the light shines in the dark they comprehend it not.

16. We call these sons Revealers of the light, but they must have the light before they can receive the light.

17. And you must teach your sons, and set their souls on fire with love and holy zeal, and make them conscious of their missions to the sons of men.

18. Teach them that Allah and man are one, but that through carnal thoughts and words and deeds, man tore himself away from Allah, debased himself.

19. Teach that the Holy Breath would make them one again, restoring harmony and peace.

20. That naught can make them one but love; that Allah so loved the world that he has clothed his son in flesh that man can comprehend.

21. The only saviour of the world is love, and Jesus, son of Mary, comes to manifest that love to men.

22. Now love cannot be manifest until its way has been prepared, and naught can rend the rock and bring down lofty hills and fill the valleys up, and thus prepare the way, but purity.

23. But purity in life men do not comprehend; and so, it, too, must come in flesh.   L

24. And you, Elizabeth, are blessed because yours is purity made flesh, and he shall pave the way for love.

25. This age will comprehend but little of the works of purity and love; but not a word is lost, for in the book of Allah's remembrance a registry is made of every thought and word and deed.

26. And when the world is ready to receive, lo, Allah will send a messenger to open the book and copy from its sacred pages all the messages of purity and love.

27. Then every man of earth will read the words of life in language of his native land, and men will see the light, and walk in the light and be the light.

28. And man again will be at one with Allah.

CHAPTER III.

ELIHU'S LESSONS—THE UNITY OF LIFE

1. Again Elihu met his pupils in the sacred grove and said:

2. No man live unto himself, for every living thing is bound by cords to every other living thing.

3. Blessed are the pure in heart; for they will love and not demand love in return.

4. They will not do to other men what they would not have other men do unto them.

5. There are two selfs; the higher and lower self.

6. The higher self is human spirit clothed with soul, made in the form of Allah.

7. The lower self, the carnal self, the body of desires, is a reflection of higher self, distorted by the murky ethers of the flesh.

8. The lower self is an illusion and will pass away; the higher self is Allah in man, and will not pass away.

9. The higher self is the embodiment of truth, the lower self is truth reversed and so is falsehood manifest.

10. The higher self is justice, mercy, love and right; the lower self is what the higher self is not.

11. The lower self breeds hatred, slander, lewdness, murders, theft and everything that harms, the higher self is mother of the virtues and the harmonies of life.

12. The lower self is rich in promises, but poor in blessedness and peace; it offers pleasure, joy and satisfying gain; but gives unrest, misery and death.

13. It gives men apples that are lovely to the eye and pleasant to the smell; their cores are full of bitterness and gall.

14. If you would ask what to study I would say, yourselves; and you well have studied them; and then would ask me what to study next, I would reply, yourselves.

15. He who knows well his lower self, knows the illusions of the world, knows of the things that pass away; and he knows his higher self, knows Allah; knows well the things that cannot pass away.

16. Thrice blessed is the man who has made purity and love his very own; he has been ransomed from the perils of the lower self and is himself his higher self.

17. Men seek salvation from an evil that deem a living monster of the neither world; and they have gods that are but demons in disguise all powerful, yet full of jealousy and hate and lust.

18. Whose favors must be bought with costly sacrifice of fruits, and of the lives of birds and animals and human kind.

19. And yet these gods possess no ears to hear, no eyes to see, no heart to sympathize, no power to save.

20. This evil is a myth; these gods are made of air, and clothed with shadows of a thought.

21. The only devil from which men must be redeemed is self, the lower self. If man would find his devil he must look within; his name is self.

22. If man would find his saviour he must look within; and when the demon self has been dethroned the saviour, love, will be exalted to the throne of power.

23. The David of the light is purity, who slays the strong Goliath of the dark, and seats the saviour, love, upon the throne.

CHAPTER IV.

DEATH AND BURIAL OF ELIZABETH—MATHENO'S LESSONS—THE MINISTRY OF DEATH

1. When John was twelve years old his mother died, and neighbors laid her body in a tomb among her kindred in the Hebron burying ground, and near the Zacharias tomb.

2. And John was deeply grieved; he wept. Matheno said, it is not well to weep because of death.

3. Death is no enemy of man; it is a friend who, when the work of life is done, just cuts the cord that binds the human boat to earth, that it may sail on smoother seas.

4. No language can desribe a mother's worth, and yours was tried and true. But she was not called hence until her tasks were done.

5. The calls of death are always for the best, for we are solving problems there as well as here; and one is sure to find himself where he can solve his problems best.

6. It is selfishness that makes one wish to call again to earth departed souls.

7. Then let your mother rest in peace. Just let her noble life be strengthened and inspiration unto you.

8. A crisis in your life has come, and you must have a clear conception of the work that you are called to do.

9. The sages of the ages call you harbinger. The Prophets look to you and say, "He is Elijah come again."

10. Your mission here is that of a harbinger; for you will go before the Messiah's face to pave his way, and make the people ready to receive their king.

11. This readiness is purity of heart; none but the pure in heart can recognize the king.

12. To teach men to be pure in heart you must yourself be pure in heart and work and deed.

13. In infancy the vow for you was made and you become a Naza-rite. The razor shall not touch your face nor head, and you shall not taste wine nor fiery drinks.

14. Men need a pattern for their lives; they love to follow, not to lead.

15. The man who stands upon the corners of the paths and points the way, but does not go, is just a pointer; and a block of wood can do the same.

16. The teacher treads the way; on every span of ground he leaves his foot-prints clearly cut, which all can see and be assured that he, their master went that way.

17. Men comprehend the inner life by what they see and do. They come to Allah through ceremonies and forms.

18. And so when they would make men know that sins are washed away by purity in life, a rite symbolic may be introduced.

19. In water wash the bodies of the people who would turn away from sin and strive for purity in life.

20. This rite of cleansing is a preparation rite and they who thus are cleansed comprised the temple of purity.

21. And you shall say, you men of Israel, hear; reform and wash; become the sons of purity, and you shall be forgiven.

22. This rite of cleansing and this temple are but symbolic of the soul, which does not come with outward show, but is the temple within.

23. Now, you may never point the way and tell the multitudes to do what you have never done; but you must go before and show the way.

24. You are to teach that men must wash; so you must lead the way, your body must be washed, symbolic of the cleansing of the soul.

25. John said, Why need I wait? May I not go at once and wash?

26. Matheno said, "'Tis well, and they went down to the Jordan ford, and east of Jerico, just where the host of Israel crossed when first they entered Canaan, they tarried for a time.

27. Matheno taught the harbinger, and he explained to him the inner meaning of the cleansing rite and how to wash himself and how to wash the multitude.

28. And in the river Jordan John was washed; then they returned unto the wilderness.

29. Now in Engedi's hills Matheno's work was done and he and John went down to Egypt. They rested unttil they reached the Temple of Sakara in the valley of the Nile.

30. For many years Matheno was a master in this temple of the Brotherhood, and when he told about the life of John and of his mission to the sons of men, the hierophant with joy received the harbinger and he was called the Brother Nazarite.

31. For eigtheen years John lived and wrought within these Temple gates; and here conquered self, became a master mind and learned the duties of the harbinger.

CHAPTER V.

After the Feast—The Homeward Journey—The Missing Jesus—The Search for Him—His Parents Find Him in the Temple—He Goes With Them to Nazareth—Symbolic Meaning of Carpenter's Tools.

1. The great Feast of the Pasch was ended and the Nazarenes were journeying toward their homes.

2. And they were in Samaria, and Mary said: Where is my son? No one had seen the boy.

3. And Joseph sought among their kindred who were on their way to Galilee; but they had seen him not.

4. Then Joseph, Mary and a son of Zebedee returned and sought through all Jerusalem, but could find him not.

5. And Mary asked the guards had they seen Jesus, a little boy about twelve years old.

6. The guards replied, yes, he is in the temple now disputing with the doctors of the law.

7. And they went in, and found him as the guards had said.

8. And Mary said, Why, Jesus, why do you treat your parents thus? Lo, we have sought two days for you. We feared that some great harm had overtaken you.

9. And Jesus said, Do you not know that I must be about my Father's work?

10. But he went round and pressed the hand of every doctor of the law and said, I trust that we meet again.

11. And then he went forth with his parents on their way to Nazareth; and when they reached their home he wrought with Joseph as a carpenter.

12. One day as he was bringing forth the tools for work he said:

13. These tools remind me of the ones we handle in the workshop of the mind where things are made of thoughts and where we build up character.

14. We use the square to measure all our lines, to straighten out the crooked places of the way, and make the corners of our conduct square.

15. We use the compass to draw the circles around our passions and desires to keep them in the bounds of righteousness.

16. We use the ax to cut away the knotty, useless and ungainly parts and make the character symmetrical.

17. We use the hammer to drive home the truth, and pound it in until it is a part of every part.

18. We use the plane to smooth the rough, uneven surface of joint, and block and board that go to build the temple for the truth.

19. The chisel, line, the plummet and the saw have all their uses in the workshop of the mind.

20. And then this ladder with its trinity of steps, faith, hope, and love; on it we climb up to the dome of purity in life.

21. And on the twelve step ladder, we ascend until we reach the pinnacle of that which life is spent to build the Temple of Perfected Man.

CHAPTER VI.

LIFE AND WORKS OF JESUS IN INDIA
AMONG THE MOSLEMS

1. A royal prince of India, Ravanna in the South, was met at the Jewish Feast.

2. Ravanna was a man of wealth, and he was just, and with a band of Brahmic priests sought wisdom in the west.

3. When Jesus stood among the Jewish priests and read and spoke, Ravanna heard and was amazed.

4. And when he asked who Jesus was, from whence he came, and what he was, Chief Hillel said:

5. We call this the day star from on high, for he has come to bring to men a light, the light of life; to lighten up the way of men and redeem his people of Israel.

6. And Hillel told Ravanna all about the child; about the prophecies concerning him; about the wonders of the night when he was born; about the visit Magian priests.

7. About the way in which he was protected from the wrath of evil men, about his flight to Egyptland, and how he then was serving with his father as a carpenter in Nazareth.

8. Ravanna was entranced, and asked to know the way to Nazareth, that he might go and honor such a one as son of Allah.

9. And with his gorgeous train he journeyed and came to Nazareth of Galilee.

10. He found the object of his search engaged in building dwelling for the sons of men.

11. And when he first saw Jesus he was climbing up a twelve step ladder, and he carried in his hands a compass, square and ax.

12. Ravanna said, All hail, most favored son of heaven!

13. And at the inn Ravanna made a feast for all the people of the town; and Jesus and his parents were the honored guests.

14. For certain days Ravanna was a guest in Joseph's home on Marmion Way; he sought to learn the secret of the wisdom of the son, but it was all too great for him.

15. And then he asked that he might be the patron of the child, might take him to the east, where he could learn the wisdom of the Brahms.

16. And Jesus longed to go, that he might learn; and after many days his parents gave consent.

17. Then, with proud heart, Ravanna, with his train, began the journey toward the rising sun; and after many days they crossed the sand and reached the provinces of Orissa, and the palace of the prince.

18. The Brahmic priests were glad to welcome home the prince; with favor they received the Jewish boy.

19. And Jesus was accepted as a pupil in the Temple of Jagaunath; and here he learned the vedas and the manic law.

20. The Brahmic Masters wondered at the clear conceptions of the child, and often were amazed when He explained to them the meaning of the law.

CHAPTER VII.

THE FRIENDSHIP OF JESUS AND LAMAAS—JESUS EXPLAINS TO LAMAAS THE MEANING OF TRUTH

1. Among the priests of Jaguanath was one who loved the Jewish boy. Lamaas Bramas was the name by which the priest was known.

2. One day as Jesus and Lamaas walked alone in plaza Jaguenath Lamaas said: "My Jewish master, what is truth?"

3. And Jesus said: "Truth is the only thing that changes not.

4. In all the world there are two things: The one is truth, the other falsehood, and falsehood that which seems to be.

5. Now the truth is aught and has no cause, and yet it is the cause of everything.

6. Falsehood is aught and yet it is the manifest of right.

7. Whatever has been made will be unmade; that which begins must end.

8. All things that can be seen by human eyes are manifests of aught. are aught, and so must pass away.

9. The things we see are but reflexes just appearing, while the ethers vibrate so and so, and when conditions change they disappear.

10. The Holy Breath is truth, is that which was, and is, and evermore shall be; it cannot change nor pass away.

11. Lamaas said: "You answer well, now what is man?"

12. And Jesus said: "Man is the truth and falsehood strangely mixed."

13. Man is the breath made flesh; so truth and falsehood are conjoined in him; and then they thrive, and naught goes down and man as truth abides."

14. Again Lamaas asked: "What do you say of power?"

15. And Jesus said: "It is a manifest; is the result of force; it is but naught; it is allusion, nothing more. Force changes not, but power changes as the ethers change."

16. "Force is the will of Allah and is omnipotent, and power is that will in manifest, directed by the Breath."

17. "There is a power in the winds, a power in the waves, a power in the lightning's stroke, a power in the human arm, a power in the eye."

18. The ethers cause these powers to be, and thought of Elohim, of angel, man, or other thinking things, directs the force; when it has done its work the power is no more."

19. Again Lamaas asked: "Of understanding, what have you to say?"

20. And Jesus said: "It is the rock on which man builds himself; it is the gnosis of the aught and of the naught, of falsehood and of truth."

21. It is the knowledge of the lower self; the sensing of the powers of man himself."

22. Again Lamaas asked: "Of wisdom, what have you to say?"

23. And Jesus said: "It is the consciousness that man is aught; that Allah and man are one."

24. That naught is naught; that power is but illusion; that heaven

and earth and hell are not above, around, below, but in; which in the light of aught becomes naught, and Allah is all.

25. Lamaas asked: "Pray what is faith?"

26. And Jesus said: "Faith is the surety of the omnipotence of Allah and man; the certainty that man will reach deific life."

27. Salvation is a ladder reaching from the heart of men to heart of Allah.

28. It has three steps: Belief is first, and this is what man thinks, perhaps, is truth.

29. And faith is next, and this is what man knows is truth.

30. Fruition is the last, and this is man himself, the truth.

31. Belief is lost in faith; and in fruition faith is lost; and man is saved when he has reached deific life; when he and Allah are one.

CHAPTER VIII.

JESUS REVEALS TO THE PEOPLE OF THEIR SINFUL WAYS

1. In all the cities of Orissa Jesus taught. At Katak, by the river side, He taught, and thousands of the people followed Him.

2. One day a car of Jaguanath was hauled along by scores of frenzied men, and Jesus said:

3. "Behold, a form without a spirit passes by; a body with no soul; a temple with no altar fires."

4. This car of Krishna is an empty thing, for Krishna is not there.

5. This car is but an idol of a people drunk on wine of carnal things.

6. Allah lives not in the noise of tongues; there is no way to Him from any idol shrine.

7. Allah's meeting place with man is in the heart, and in a still small voice he speaks; and he who hears is still ill.

8. And all the people said: "Teach us to know the Holy One who speaks within the heart, Allah of the still small voice."

9. And Jesus said: "The Holy Breath cannot be seen with mortal eyes; nor can men see the spirit of the Holy One."

10. But in their image man was made, and he who looks into the face of man, looks at the image of Allah who speaks within.

11. And when man honors man he honors Allah, and what man does for man, he does for Allah.

12. And you must bear in mind that when man harms in thought or word or deed another man, he does a wrong to Allah.

13. If you would serve Allah who speaks within the heart, just serve your near of kin, and those who are no kin, the stranger at your gates, the foe who seeks to do you harm.

14. Assist the poor, and help the weak; do harm to none and covet not what is not yours.

15. Then, with your tongue the Holy One will speak; and he will smile behind your tears, will light your countenance with joy, and fill your hearts with peace.

16. And then the people asked, "To whom shall we bring gifts? Where shall we offer sacrifice?"

17. And Jesus said, "Our Father—Allah asks not for needless waste of plant, of grain, of dove, of lamb."

18. That which you burn on any shrine you throw away. No blessing can attend the one who takes the food from hungry mouths to be destroyed by fire.

19. When you would offer sacrifice unto Allah, just take your gift of grain, or meat, and lay it on the table of the poor.

20. From it an incense will arise to heaven, which will return to you with blessedness.

21. Tear down your idols; they can hear you not; turn all your sacrificed altars into fuel for the flames.

22. Make human hearts your altars, and burn your sacrifices with the fire of love.

23. And all the people were entranced, and would have Jesus as a God; but Jesus said:

24. "I am your brother man, just come to show the way to Allah; you shall not worship man; praise Allah the Holy One."

CHAPTER IX

JESUS ATTENDS A FEAST IN BEHAR AND HERE HE TAUGHT HUMAN EQUALITY

1. The fame of Jesus as a teacher spread through all the land, and people came from near and far to hear his words of truth.

2. At Behar, on the sacred river of the Brahms, he taught for many days.

3. And Ach, a wealthy man of Behar, made a feast in honor of his guests and he invited every one to come.

4. And many came; among them thieves, extortioners and courtesans, and Jesus sat with them and taught; but they who followed him were much aggrieved, because He sat with thieves and courtesans.

5. And they upbraided Him; they said, "Robboni, Master of the wise, this day will be an evil day for you.

6. "The news will spread that you consort with courtesans and men will shun you as they shun an asp."

7. And Jesus answered them and said, "A master never screens Himself for the sake of reputation or of fame."

8. These are but worthless baubles of the day; they arise and sink, like empty bottles on a stream; they are illusions and will pass away.

9. They are the indices to what the thoughtless think; they are noise that people make; and shallow men judge merit by the noise.

10. Allah and all master men judge men by what they are and not what they seem to be; not by their reputation and their fame.

11. These courtesans and thieves are children of my Father, Allah; their souls are just as precious in His sight as yours; or of the Brahmic priests.

12. And they are working out the same life sums that you have solved, you men who look at them with scorn.

13. And some of them have solved much harder than you have solved, you men who look at them with scorn.

14. Yes, they are sinners, and confess their guilt while you are guilty, but are shrewd enough to have a polished coat to cover up your guilt.

15. Suppose you men who scorn the courtesans, these drunkards and these thieves, who know that you are pure in heart and life, that you are better far than they, stand forth that man know just who you are.

16. The sin lies in the wish, in the desire, not in the act.

17. You covet other people's wealth; you look at charming forms, and deep within your heart you lust for them.

18. Deceit you practice every day, and wish for gold, for honor and for fame, just for your selfish selves.

19. The man who covet is a thief, and she who lust is courtesan. You who are none of these speak out.

20. Nobody spoke; the accusers held their peace.

21. And Jesus said, "The proof this day is all against those who have accused."

22. The pure in heart do not accuse. The vile in heart who want to cover up their guilt with holy smoke of piety are never loathing drunkards, thieves and courtesans.

23. This loathing and this scorn is mockery, for if the tinseled coat of reputation could be torn away, the loud professor would be found to reveal in his lust, deceit and many forms of secret sin.

24. The man who spends his time in pulling other people's weeds can have no time in pulling his own, and all the choicest flowers of life will be choked and die, and nothing will remain but darnal, thistles and burs.

25. And Jesus spoke a parable; He said, Behold a farmer had great fields of ripened grain, and when he looked he saw that blades of many stalks of wheat were bent and broken down.

26. And when he sent his reapers forth he said, we will not save the stalks of wheat that have the broken blades.

27. Go forth and cut and burn the stalks with broken blades.

28. And after many days he went to measure up his grain, but not a kernel could he find;

29. And then he called the harvesters and said to them, where is my grain?

30. They answered him and said we did according to your word; we gathered up and burned the stalks with broken blades, and not a stalk was left to carry to the barn.

31. And Jesus said, if Allah saves only those who have broken blades, who have been perfected in his sight, who will be saved?

32. And the accusers hung their heads in shame; and Jesus went his way.

CHAPTER X.

JESUS SPAKE ON THE UNITY OF ALLAH
AND MAN TO THE HINDUS

1. Benares in the sacred city of the Brahms, and in Benares. Jesus taught; Udraka was his host.

2. Udraka made a feast in honor of his guests, and many high born Hindu priests and scribes were there.

3. And Jesus said to him, with much delight, I speak to you concerning life—the brotherhood of life.

4. The universal Allah is one, yet he is more than one; all things are one.

5. By the sweet breath of Allah all life is bound in one; so if you touch a fiber of a living thing you send a thrill from center to the outer bounds of life.

6. And when you crush beneath your foot the meanest worm, you shake the throne of Allah and cause the sword of life to tremble in its sheath.

7. The birds sing out its song for men, and men vibrate in unison to help it sing.

8. The ant constructs its home, the bee its sheltering comb, the spider weaves her web and bowers breathe to them a spirit in their sweet perfume that gives them strength to toil.

9. Now, men and birds and beasts and creeping things are deities, made flesh; and how dare you kill anything?

10. It is cruelty that makes the world awry when men have learned that when they harm a living thing, they harm themselves, they surely will not kill, nor cause a thing that Allah has made to suffer pain.

11. A lawyer said, I pray to Jesus, tell who is this Allah you speak about; where are his priests, his temples and his shrines?

12. And Jesus said, the Allah I speak about is everywhere; He cannot be compassed with walls, nor hedged about with bounds of any kind.

13. All people worship Allah, the One; but all the people see Him not alike.

14. This universal Allah is wisdom, will and love.

15. All men see not the Triune Allah. One sees Him as Allah of might, another as Allah of thought, another as Allah of love.

16. A man's ideal is his God and so, as man unfolds, his God unfolds. Man's God to-day, to-morrow is not God.

17. The nation of the earth see Allah from different point of view, and so he does not seem the same to every one.

18. Man name the part of Allah he sees, and this to him is all of Allah; and every nation sees a part of Allah, and every nation had a name for Allah.

19. You Brahmans call him Parabrahm, in Egypt He is Troth, and Jens is His name in Greece, Johovah is His Hebrew name, but every-

where he is the causeless cause, the rootless root from which all things have grown.

20. When men afraid of Allah, and take Him for a foe, they dress up other men in fancy garbs and call them priests.

21. And charge them to restrain the wrath of Allah by prayers, and when they fail to win His favor by their prayers, to buy Him off with sacrifice of animals or birds.

22. When man sees Allah as one with him, as Father Allah he needs no middle man, no priest to intercede.

23. He goes straight up to Him and says, my Father God, Allah! And then he lays his hands in Allah's own hand, and all is well.

24. And this is Allah. You are, each one, a priest, just for yourself; and sacrifice of blood Allah does not want.

25. Just give your life in sacrificial service to the all of life and Allah is pleased.

26. When Jesus had thus said He stood aside; the people were amazed, but strove among themselves.

27. Some said, He is inspired by Holy Brahm and others said He is insane, and others said He is obsessed; He speaks as devils speak.

28. But Jesus tarried not. Among the guests was one, a tiller of the soil, a generous soul, a seeker after truth, who loved the words that Jesus spoke, and Jesus went with him and in his home abode.

CHAPTER XI.

JESUS AND BARATA—TOGETHER THEY READ THE SACRED BOOKS

1. Among the Buddhists preists was one who saw a lofty wisdom in the words that Jesus spoke. It was Barato Arabo.

2. Together Jesus and Barato read the Jewish Psalms and prophets, read the vedas, and Avesta and the wisdom of Guatama.

3. And as they read and talked about the possibilities of man, Barato said: Man is the marvel of the universe. He is a part of everything, for he has been a living thing on every plane of life.

5. Time was when man was not, and then he was a bit of formless substance in the molds of time, and then a protoplast.

6. By universal law all things tend upward to a state of perfectness. The protoplast evolved, becoming worm, then reptile, bird and beast, and then at last it reached the form of man.

7. Now, man himself is mind, and mind is here to gain perfection by experience; and mind is often manifest in fleshy form, and in the form best suited to its growth. So mind may manifest as worm, or bird or beast or man.

8. The time will come when everything of life will be evolved unto the state of perfect man.

9. And after man is man in perfectness, he will evolve to higher forms of life.

10. And Jesus said, Barata Arabo, who told you this, that mind, which is man, may manifest in flesh of beast or bird or creeping thing?

11. Barata said, from time which man remembers not our priests have told us so, and so we know.

12. And Jesus said, enlighten Arabo, are you a master mind and do not know that man knows naught by being told?

13. Man may believe what others say, but thus he never knows. If man would know, he must, himself, be what he knows.

14. Do you remember, Arabo, when you was ape, or bird, or worm?

15. Now, if you have no better proving of your plea than that the priests have told you so, you do not know; you simply guess.

16. Regard not, then, what any man has said; let us forget the flesh and go with mind into the land of fleshless things; mind never does forget.

17. And backward thruogh the ages master minds can trace themselves; and thus they know.

18. Time never was when man was not.

19. That which begins will have an end. If man was not, the time will come when he will not exist.

20. From Allah's own record book we read: The Triune Allah breathed forth, and stood seven spirits his face. The Hebrews call these seven spirits Elohim.

21. And these are they who, in their boundless power, created everything that is, or was.

22. These spirits of the Triune Allah moved on the face of boundless space and seven others were and every other had its form of life.

23. These forms of life were but the thought of Allah, clothed in the substance of their ether planes.

24. Men call these ether planes, the planes of protoplast, of earth, of plant, of beast, of man, of angel and cherubim.

25. These planes with all their teeming thoughts of Allah are never seen by eyes of man in flesh; they are composed of substance far too fine for fleshy eyes to see, and still they constitute the soul of things.

26. And with the eyes of soul all creatures see these ether planes, and all the forms of life.

27. Because all forms of life on every plane are thoughts of Allah, all creatures think, and every creature is possessed of will, and in its measure, has the power to choose.

28. And in their native planes all creatures are supplied with nourishment from the ethers of their planes.

29. And so it was with every living thing until the will became a sluggish will, and then the ethers of the protoplast, the earth, the plant, the beast, the man, began to vibrate very slow.

30. The ethers became more dense, and all the creatures of these planes were clothed with coarser garbs of flesh, which men can see; and thus the coarser manifest, which men call physical, appeared.

31. And this is what is called the fall of man; but man fell not alone for protoplast, and earth, and plant and beast were all included in the fall.

32. The angels and the cherubim fell not; their will were never strong, and so they held the ethers of their planes in harmony with Allah.

33. Now, when the ether reached the rate of atmosphere, and all the creatures of these planes must get their food from atmosphere, the conflict came; and then that which the finite man called survival of the best, became a law.

34. The stronger ate the bodies of the weaker manifests; and here is where the carnal of evolution had its rise.

35. And now man, in his utter shamelessness, strikes down and eats the beasts, the beasts consume the plant, the plant thrives on the earth, the earth absorbs the protoplast.

36. In yonder kingdom of the soul this carnal evolution is not known, and the great work of master minds is to restore the heritage of man, to bring him back to his estate that he had lost, when he again will live upon the ethers of his native plane.

37. The thoughts of Allah change not; the manifests of life on every plane unfolds into perfection of their kind; and as the thought of Allah can never die, there is not death to any being of the seven ethers of the seven spirits of the Triune Allah.

38. And so an earth is never plant; a beast or bird, or creeping thing is never man, and man is not, and cannot be, a beast, or bird, or creeping thing.

39. The time will come when all these manifests will be absorbed, and man and beast and plant and earth and protoplast will be redeemed.

40. Barata was amazed; the wisdom of the Jewish sage was revelation unto him.

41. Now, Vidyapati, wisest of the Indian sages, chief of the temple Kapavistu, heard Barata speak to Jesus of the origin of man, and heard the answer of the Hebrew prophet, and he said:

42. You priests of Kapavistu, hear me speak; we stand today upon a crest of time. Six time ago a master soul was born who gave a glorious light to man, and now a master sage stands in the temple Kapavistu.

43. The Hebrew prophet is the rising star of wisdom, deified. He brings to us a knowledge of the secret things of Allah; and all the world will hear his words, and glorify his name.

44. You priests of temple Kapavistu, stay; be still and listen when he speaks; he is the living Oracle of Allah.

35. And all the priests gave thanks, and praised the Buddha of enlightenment.

CHAPTER XII.

JESUS TEACHES THE COMMON PEOPLE AT A SPRING— TELLS THEM HOW TO OBTAIN ETERNAL HAPPINESS

1. In silent meditation Jesus sat beside a flowing spring. It was a holy day, and many people of the servant caste were near the place.

2. And Jesus saw the hard drawn lines of toil on every brow, in every hand. There was no look of joy in any face. Not one of all the group could think of anything but toil.

3. And Jesus spoke to one and said, "Why are you all so sad? Have you no happiness in life?"

4. The man replied, "We scarcely, We scarcely know the meaning of that word. We toil to live, and hope for nothing else but toil, and bless the day when we can cease our toil and lay down and rest in Buddah's city of the dead."

5. And Jesus's heart was stirred with pity and with love for these poor toilers, and he said:

6. "Toil should not make a person sad; men should be happiest when they toil. When hope and love are back of toil, then all of life is filled with joy and peace, and this is heaven. Do you not know that such a heaven is for you?"

7. The man replied, "Of heaven we have heard; but when it is so far away, and we must live so many lives before we reach that place!"

8. "And Jesus said, "My brother man, your thoughts are wrong; your heaven is not far away, and it is not a place of metes and bounds, is not a country to be reached; it is a state of mind!"

9. Allah never made a heaven for man; he never made a hell; we are creators and make our own.

10. Now, cease to seek for heaven in the sky; just open up the windows of your hearts, and, like a flood of light, a heaven will come and bring a boundless joy; then the toil will be no cruel task.

11. The people were amazed, and gathered close to hear this strange young master speak.

12. Imploring him to tell them more about the Father God, Allah, about the heaven that men can make on earth, about the boundless joy.

13. And Jesus spake a parable; He said, "A certain man possessed a field; the soil was hard and poor.

14. "By constant toil he scarcely could provide enough food to keep his family from want.

15. "One, day a miner who could see beneath the soil, in passing on his way, saw this poor man and his unfruitful field.

16. "He called the weary toiler and said, "My brother, know you not that just below the surface of your barren field rich treasures lie concealed?

17. You plow and sow and reap in a scanty way, and day by day you tread upon a mine of gold and precious stones.

18. "This wealth lies not upon the surface of the ground; but if you will but dig away the rocky soil; and delve down deep into the earth, you need no longer till the soil for naught."

19. "The man believed. "The miner surely knows," "And I will find the treasures hidden in my field."

20. "And then he dug away the rocky soil, and deep down in the earth he found a mine of gold."

21. And Jesus said, "The sons of men are toiling hard on desert plains, and burning sands and rocky soils, are doing what their fathers did, not dreaming that they can do aught else."

22. Behold a master comes, and tells them of a hidden wealth; that underneath the rocky soil of carnal things are treasures that no man can count.

23. That in the heart the richest gems abound; that he who wills may open the door and find them all.

24. And then the people said, "Make known to us the way that we may find the wealth that lies within the heart."

25. And Jesus opened up the way; the toilers saw another side of life, and toil became a joy.

CHAPTER XIII.

LIFE AND WORKS OF JESUS IN EGYPT AMONG THE GENTILES.

1. Jesus with Elihu and Salome in Egypt. Tells the story of His journeys. Elihu and Salome praise Allah. Jesus goes to the temple in Helipolis and is received as a pupil.

2. And Jesus came to Egyptland, and all was well. He tarried not upon the coast; He went at once to Zoan, home of Elihu and Salome, who five and twenty years before had taught his mother in their Sacred school.

3. And there was joy when met these three. When last the son of Mary saw these sacred groves he was a babe.

4. And now a man grown strong by buffeting of every kind; a teacher who had stirred the multitudes in many lands.

5. And Jesus told the aged teachers all about His life; about His journeyings in foreign lands; about the meetings with the masters and His kind receptions by the multitudes.

6. Elihu and Salome heard His story with delight; they lifted up their eyes to heaven and said:
"Our Father-God Allah, let now Thy servants go in peace; for we have seen the glory of Allah."

7. And we have talked with Him, the messenger of love, and of the covenant of peace on earth, good will to men.

8. Through Him shall all the nations of the earth be blessed, thru Him, Immanuel.

9. And Jesus stayed in Zoan many days; and then went forth into the city of the sun, that men called Helipolis, and sought admission to the temple of the sacred brotherhood.

10. The council of the brotherhood convened, and Jesus stood before the hierophant; He answered all questions that were asked with clearness and with power.

11. The hierophant exclaimed, "Rabboni of the rabbinate, why come you here? Your wisdom is the wisdom of the gods. Why seek for wisdom in the halls of men?

12. And Jesus said, in every way of life I would walk; in every hall of learning I would sit; the heights that any man has gained, these I would gain.

13. What any man has suffered I would meet, that I may know the griefs, the disappointments and the sore temptations of my brother man; that I may know just how to succor those in need.

14. I pray you brothers, let me go into your dismal crypts; and I would pass the hardest of your tests.

15. The master said. "Take then the vow of secret brotherhood." And Jesus took the vow of secret brotherhood.

16. Again the master spoke; he said: "The greatest heights are

gained by those who reach the greatest depths; and you shall reach the greatest depths."

17.   The guide then led the way and in the fountain Jesus bathed; and when he had been clothed in proper garb he stood again before the hierophant.

CHAPTER XIV.

THE MINISTRY OF JOHN THE HARBINGER

John the Harbinger, returns to Hebron, lives as a hermit in the wilds, visits Jerusalem and speaks to the people.

1.   It came to pass when John, the son of Zacharias and Elizabeth, had finished all his studies in the Egyptian schools he returned to Hebron, where he abode for certain days.

2.   And then he sought the wilderness and made his home in David's cave, where many years before he was instructed by the Egyptian sages.

3.   Some people called him the Hermit of Engedi; and others said, he is the wild man of the hills.

4.   He clothed himself with skins of the beasts; his food was carobs, honey, nuts and fruits.

5.   When John was thirty years of age he went into Jerusalem, and in the market place he sat in silence seven days.

6.   The common people and the priests, the scribes and the Pharisees came out in multitudes to see the silent hermit of the hills; but none were bold enough to ask him who he was.

7.   But when his silent past was done, he stood forth in the midst of all and said:

8.   Behold the King has come; the prophets told of Him; the wise men long have looked for Him.

9.   "Prepare, O Israel, prepare to meet your King."

10.   And that was all he said, and then he disappeared, and no one knew where he had gone. -

11.   And there was great unrest through all Jerusalem. The rulers heard the story of the hermit of the hills.

12.   And they sent couriers forth to talk with him that they might know about the coming King; but they could find him not.

13.   And after certain days he came again into the market place, and all the city came to hear him speak. He said:

14.   Be not disturbed, you rulers of the state; the coming King is no antagonist; He seeks no place on earthly throne.

15.   "The eyes of men shall see it not and none can enter but the pure in heart.

16.   "Prepare, O Israel, prepare to meet your King."

17.   Again the hermit disappeared; the people strove to follow him, but he drew a veil about his form and men could see him not.

18.   Jewish feast day came; Jerusalem was filled with Jews and proselytes from every part of Palestine and John stood in the temple court and said:

19.   "Prepare, O Israel, prepare to meet your King."

20.   So, you have lived in sin; the poor cry in your streets, and you regard them not.

21. Your neighbors, who are they? You have defrauded friends and foes alike.

22. You worship Allah with voice and lip; your hearts are far away, and set on gold.

23. Your priests have bound upon the people burdens far too great to bear; they live in ease upon the hard earned wages of the poor.

24. Your lawyers, doctors, scribes, are useless cumberers of the ground; they are but tumors on the body of the state.

25. They toil not, neither do they spin, yet they consume the profits of your marts of trade.

26. Your rulers are adulterers, extortioners and thieves, regarding not the rights of man.

27. And robbers ply their calling in the sacred hills; the holy temple you have sold to thieves; their dens are in the sacred places set apart for prayer.

28. Hear! Hear! You people of Jerusalem! Reform: turn from your evil ways or Allah will turn from you, and heathen from afar will come, and what is left of all your honor and your fame will pass in one short hour.

29. Prepare, Jerusalem, prepare to meet your King.

30. He said no more; he left the court and no one saw him go.

31. The priests, the doctors and the scribes were all in rage. They sought for John, intent to do him no harm. They found him not.

CHAPTER XV.

Divine Ministry of Jesus—Jesus Goes to the Wilderness for Self-Examination, Where He Remains Forty Days. Is Subjected to Three Temptations—He Overcomes. Returns to the Camps of John and Begins Teaching

1. The harbinger had paved the way; the Logos had been introduced to men as love made manifest, and he must now begin his divine ministry.

2. And He went forth into the wilderness to be alone with Allah, that He might look into His inner heart, and note its strength and worthiness.

3. And with Himself He talked; He said, "My lower self is strong; by many ties I am bound down to carnal life.

4. "Have I the strength to overcome and give my life a willing sacrifice for men?

5. "When I shall stand before the face of men, and they demand a proof of my Messiahship, what will I say?"

6. And then the tempter came and said, "If you be the Son of Allah, command these stones to turn to bread."

7. And Jesus said, "Who is it that demands a test? It is no sign that one is a Son of Allah because he does a miracle; the devils can do mighty things.

8. "Did not the Gentiles magicians do great things before the Pharoah?

9. "My words and deeds in all the walks of life shall be the proof of my Messiahship."

10. And then the tempter said, "If you will go into Jerusalem and

from the temple pinnacle cast down yourself to earth, the people will believe you are the Messiah sent from Allah.

11. This you can surely do; for did not David say, "He gives His angels charge concerning you, and with their hands will they uphold lest you shall fall?"

12. And Jesus said, "I will not tempt the Lord, my God, Allah."

13. And then the tempter said, "Look forth upon the world; behold its honors and its fame! Behold its pleasures and its wealth.

14. "If you will give your life to these they shall be yours."

15. But Jesus said, "Away fom me all tempting thoughts. My heart is fixed. I spurn this carnal self with all its vain ambition and its pride."

16. For forty days did Jesus wrestle with his carnal self ;His higher self prevailed. He then was hungry, but his friends had found Him and they ministered to Him.

17. Then Jesus left the wilderness, and in the consciousness of Holy Breath, He came into the camps of John and taught.

CHAPTER XVI

Pilate's Final Effort to Release Jesus Fails—He Washes His Hands in Feigned Innocence—Delivers Jesus to the Jews for Execution— The Soldiers Drive Him to Calvary

1. A superstitious people are the Jews. They have a faith that they have borrowed from the idol worshippers of other lands, that at the end of every year.

2. They may heap all their sins upon the head of some man set apart to bear their sins.

3. The man becomes a scape goat for the multitudes; and they believed that when they drive him forth into the wilds, or into foreign lands, they are released from sins.

4. So every spring before the feast they chose a prisoner from the prisons of the land, and by a form of their own, they fain would make him bear their sins away.

5. Among the Jewish prisoners in Jerusalem were three who were the leaders of a vile, seditious band, who had engaged in thefts and murders and rapine, and had been sentenced to be crucified.

6. Barabbas and Jezia was among the men who were to die, but he was rich and he had bought off priests the boon to be the scape goat for the people at the coming feast, and he was anxiously in waiting for his hour to come.

7. Now, Pilate thought to turn his superstition to account to save the Lord Jesus, and so he went before the Jews and said:

8. "You men of Israel, according to my custom, I will release to you today a prisoner who shall bear your sins away.

9. "This man you drive into the wilds or in foreign lands, and you have asked me to release Barabbas, who has been proven guilty of the murder of a score of men.

10. Now, hear me men. Let Jesus be released and let Barabbas pay his debt upon the cross; then you can send this Jesus to the wilds and hear no more of Him.

11. At what the ruler said the people were enraged, and they began to plot to tear the Roman palace down and drive in exile Pilate and his Household and his guards.

12. When Pilate was assured that Civil War would follow if he heeded not to the wishes of the mob, he took a bowl of water and in the presence of the multitude he washed his hands and said:

13. This man whom you accuse is Son of the Most High Allah, and I proclaim my innocence.

14. "If you would shed His blood, His blood is on your hands and not mine."

15. And then the Jews exclaimed, "And let His blood be on our hands and on our children's hands."

16. And Pilate trembled like a leaf, in fear. Barabbas he released, and as the Lord stood forth before the mob, the ruler said, "Behold your King! And would you put to death your King?"

17. The Jews replied, "He is no King; we have no King by great Tiberius."

18. Now, Pilate would not give consent that Roman soldiers should imbue their hands in blood of innocence, and so the chief priests and the Pharises took council what to do with Jesus.

19. Caiap has said, "We cannot crucify this man. He must be stoned to death and nothing more."

20. And then the rabble said, "Make haste! Let Him be stoned." And then they led Him forth toward the hill beyond the city's gates where criminals were put to death.

21. The rabble could not wait until they reached the place of skulls. As soon as they had passed the city's gates, they rushed upon Him, smote Him with their hands, they spit upon Him, stoned Him and He fell upon the ground.

22. And one, a man of Allah, stood forth and said, He shall be bruised for our transgressions and by His stripes we shall be healed."

23. And Jesus laid all bruised and mangled on the ground, a High Priest called out, "Stay, stay, you men! Behold the guards of Herod come and they will crucify this man."

24. And there beside the city's gates they found Barabbas's cross, and then the frenzied mob cried out, "Let Him be crucified."

25. Caiaphas and the other ruling Jews came forth and gave consent.

26. And they lifted Jesus from the ground, and at the point of swords they drove Him on.

27. A man named Simon, from Cyrene, a friend of Jesus, was near the scene, and since the bruised and wounded Jesus could not bear His cross, they laid it on the shoulders of this man, and made him bear it to Calvary.

CHAPTER XVII.

Jesus Appears, Fully Materialized, Before Apollo and the Silent Brotherhood in Greece—Appears to Claudas and Juliet on Tiber Near Rome—Appears to the Priests in the Egyptian Temple at Heliopolis

1. Apollo, with the Silent Brotherhood of Greece, was sitting in a delphian grove. The Oracle had spoken loud and long.

2. The priests were in the sanctuary as they looked the Oracle became a blaze of light; it seemed to be on fire, and all consumed.

3. The priests were filled with fear. They said a great disaster is to come; our gods are mad; they have destroyed our Oracle.

4. But when the flames had spent themselves, a man stood on the Oracle pedestal and said:

5. "Allah speaks to man, not by an oracle of wood and gold, but by the voice of man."

6. "The gods have spoken to the Greeks, and kindred tongues, through image made by man, but Allah the One, now speaks to man through Jesus the only Son, who was and is and evermore will be.

7. "This Oracle will fail; the living Oracle of Allah, the One, will not fail."

8. Apollo knew the man who spoke; he knew it was the Nazarene who once had taught the wise men in the Acropolis and had rebuked the idol worshippers upon the Athen's beach.

9. And in a moment Jesus stood before Apollo and the Silent Brotherhood and said:

10. "Behold, for I have risen from the dead with gifts for men. I bring to you the title of your vast estate.

11. "All power in heaven and earth is mine; to you I give all power in heaven and earth."

12. "Go forth and teach the nations of the earth the Gospel of the resurrection of the dead and eternal life through Jesus, the love of Allah made manifest to men."

13. And then he clasped Apollo's hand and said: "My human flesh was changed to higher form by love divine and I can manifest in flesh or in the higher planes of life at will."

14. "What I can do all men can do. Go teach the Gospel of the Omnipotence of men."

15. Then Jesus disappeared; but Greece and Crete and all the nations heard.

16. Claudas and Juliet, his wife, lived on the palatine in Rome and they were servants of Tiberius; but they had been in Galilee.

17. Had walked with Jesus by the sea, had heard his words and seen his power; and they believed that he was Jesus made manifest.

18. Now Claudas and his wife were on the Tiber in a little boat; a storm swept from the sea, and the boat was wrecked and Claudas and his wife were sinking down to death.

19. And Jesus came and took them by the hands and said: "Claudas and Juliet, arise and walk with me upon the waves."

20. And they arose and walked with Him upon the waves,

21. A thousand people saw three walk on the waves, and saw them reach the land, and they were all amazed.

22. And Jesus said: "You men of Rome, I am the resurrection and the life. They that are dead shall live, and many that shall live will never die."

23. By mouth of gods and demigods Allah spoke unto your fathers long ago; but now He speaks to you through perfect man."

24. "He sent his son, Jesus in human flesh to save the world, and as I lifted from the watery grave and saved these servants of Tiberius."

25. "So Jesus will lift the sons and daughters of the human race, yea every one of them, from darkness and from graves of carnal things to light and everlasting life.

26. "I am the manifest of love raised from the dead; behold my hands, my feet, my side which carnal men have pierced.

27. "Claudas and Juliet, whom I have saved from death, are my ambassadors to Rome.

28. "And they will point the way and teach the Gospel of the Holy Breath and the resurrection of the dead."

29. And that was all He said, but Rome and all of Italy heard.

30. The priests of Heliopolis were in their temple met to celebrate the resurrection of their brother Nazarite; they knew that he had risen from the dead.

31. The Nazarite appeared and stood upon a sacred pedestal on which no man had ever stood.

32. This was an honor that had been reserved for him who first would demonstrate the resurrection of the dead.

33. When Jesus stood upon the sacred pedestal the masters stood and said: "All hail!" The great bells of the temple rang and all the temple was ablaze with light.

35. And Jesus said: "All honor to the masters of this Temple of the Sun."

35. In flesh of man there is the essence of the resurrection of the dead. This essence quickened by the Holy Breath, will raise the substance of the Body to higher tone.

36. And make it like the substance of the bodies of the planes above, which human eyes cannot behold.

37. There is a holy ministry in death. The essence of the body cannot be quickened by the Holy Breath until the fixed is solved; the body must disintegrate, and this is death.

38. And then upon these pliant substance Allah breathes, just as he breathed upon the chaos of the deep when the worlds were formed.

39. And life springs forth from death; the carnal form is changed to form divine.

40. The will of man makes possible the action of the Holy Breath. When will of man and will of Allah are one, the resurrection is a fact.

41. In this we have the chemistry of mortal life, the ministry of death, the mystery of deific life.

42. My human form was wholly given to bring my will to tune with the deific will; when this was done by earth-tasks all were done.

43. And you, my brothers, know full well the foes I had to meet; you know about my victories in Gethsemane; my trials in the courts of men; my death upon the cross.

44. You know that all my life was one great drama for the sons of men; a pattern for the sons of men. I have lived to show the possibilities of man.

45. What I have done all men can do, and what I am all men shall be.

46. The masters looked; the form upon the sacred pedestal had gone, but every temple priest, and every living creature said, praise Allah.

CHAPTER XVIII

The Resurrection of Jesus—Pilate Places the Roman Seal Upon the Stone Door of the Tomb—At Midnight a Company of the Silent Brothers March About the Tomb—The Soldiers are Alarmed— Jesus Teaches to the Spirits in Prison—Early Sunday Morning He Rises from the Tomb. The Soldiers are Bribed by the Priests to Say that the Disciples Had Stolen the Body.

1. The tomb in which they laid the body of the Lord was in a garden, rich with flowers, the garden of Saloam, and Joseph's home was near.

2. Before the watch began Caiaphas sent a company of priests out to the garden of Saloam that they might be assured that Jesus body was within the tomb.

3. They rolled the stone away; they saw the body there, and then they placed the stone again before the door.

4. And pilate sent his scribe who placed upon the stone the seal of Rome, in such a way that he who moved it would break the seal.

5. To break this Roman seal meant death to him who broke the seal.

6. The Jewish soldiers all were sworn to faithfulness; and then the watch began.

7. At midnight all were well, but suddenly the tomb became a blaze of light, and down the garden walked a troupe of white claid soldiers marched in single file.

8. They came up to the tomb and marched and countermarched before the door.

9. The Jewish soldiers were alert; they thought his friends had come to steal the body of the Nazarene. The captain of the guard cried out to charge.

10. They charged; but not a white clad soldier fell. They did not even stop; they marched and counter-marched among the frightened men.

11. They stood upon the Roman seal; they did not speak; they unsheathed not their swords; it was the Silent Brotherhood.

12. The Jewish soldiers fled in fear; they fell upon the ground.

13. They stood apart until the white clad soldiers marched away and then the light about the tomb grew dim.

14. Then, they returned; the stone was in its place; the seal was not disturbed, and they resumed their march.

15. Now, Jesus did not sleep within the tomb, The body is manifest of soul; but soul is without its manifest.

16. And in the realm of souls unmanifest, the Lord went and taught.

17. He opens up the prison doors and set the prisoners free.

18. He broke the chain of captive souls, and let the captives to the light.

19. He sat in council with the patriarchs and prophets of the olden times.

20. The masters of all times and climes He met, and in the great assemblies He stood forth and told the story of His life on earth, and of his death in sacrifice for man.

21. And of his promises to clothe himself again in garb of flesh and walk with His disciples, just to prove the possibilities of man.

22. To give to them the key of life, of death and of the resurrection of the dead.

23. In council all the masters sat and talked about the revelations of the coming age.

24. When she, the Holy Breath, shall fill the earth and air with holy breath and open up the way of man to perfectness and endless life.

25. The garden of Saloam was silent on the Sabbath day. The Jewish soldiers watched and no one else approached the tomb; but on the following night the scene was changed.

26. At midnight every Jewish soldier heard a voice which said: "Adon Mashich Cumi," which meant, Lord Jesus arise."

27. And they supposed again the friends of Jesus were alert, were coming up to take the body of their Lord away.

28. The soldiers were alert with swords unseathed and drawn, and then they heard the words again.

29. It seemed as thought the voice was everywhere, and yet they saw no man.

30. The soldiers blanched with fear, and still to flee meant death for cowardice, and so they stood and watched.

31. Again, all this was before the sun arose, the heavens blaze with light; a distant thunder seemed to herald forth a coming storm.

32. And then the earth began to quake and in the rays of light they saw a form descend from heaven. They said: "Behold, an Angel comes."

33. And then they heard again, "Adon Mashich Cumi."

34. And then the white-robed form tramped on the Roman seal, and then he tore it into shreds; he took the mighty stone in his hand as though it were a pebble from the brook, and cast it to the side.

35. And Jesus opened His eyes and said: "All hail the rising sun; the coming of the day of righteousness!"

36. And then he folded up his buriel gown, his head bands and his coverings and laid them all aside.

37. He rose, and for a moment stood beside the white-robed form.

38. The weaker soldiers fell to the ground and hid their faces in their hands; the stronger stood and watched.

39. They saw the body of the Nazarene transmute. They saw it change from mortal to immortal form, and then it disappeared.

40. The soldiers heard a voice from everywhere; yet, from everywhere, it said:

41. Peace, peace on earth good will to men.

42. They looked, the tomb was empty and the Lord had risen as He said.

43. The soldiers hastened to Jerusalem, and to the priests, and said:

44. "Behold the Nazarene has arisen as He said; the tomb is empty and the body of the man is gone; we know not where it is. And then they told about the wonders of the night.

45. Caiaphas called a council of the Jews; he said, "The news must not go forth that Jesus has arisen from the dead.

46. "For if it does, all men will say, "He is the Son of Allah, and our testimonies will be proven false."

47. And then they called the hundred soldiers in and said to them:

48. "You know not where the body of the Nazarene is resting now, so if you will go forth and say that His disciples came and stole the body while you slept.

49. "Each one of you shall have a silver piece, and we will make it right with Pilate for the breaking of the Roman seal."

50. The soldiers did as they were paid to do.

CHAPTER XIX

Jesus Appears, Fully Materialized, to the Eastern Sages in the Palace of Prince Ravanna in India—To the Magician Priests in Persia— Three Wise Men Speak in Praise of the Personality of the Nazarene.

1. Ravanna, prince of India, gave a feast. His palace in Orissa was the place where the men of thought from all the farther East were want to meet.

2. Ravanna was the prince with whom the child Jesus went to India with when twelve years old.

3. The feast was made in honor of the wise men of the East.

4. Among the guests were Mangste, Vidyapati, and Lamaas.

5. The wise men sat about the table talking about the needs of India and the world.

6. The door unto the banquet hall was in the East; a vacant chair was at the table to the East.

7. And as the wise men talked a stranger entered, unannounced, and raising up his hands in benediction, said, "All hail!"

8. A halo rested on his head, and light, unlike the light of sun, filled all the room.

10. And Jesus sat down in the vacant chair and then the wise men knew it was the Gentile prophet who had come.

11. And Jesus said, "Behold, for I am risen from the dead, look at my hands, my feet, my side.

12. The Roman soldiers pierced my hands and feet with nails; and then one pierced my heart.

13. "They put Me in a tomb, and then I wrestled with the conqueror of men. I conquered death, I stamped upon him and rose.

14. "Brought immortality to light and painted on the walls of time a rainbow for the sons of men; and what I did all men shall do.

15. The gospel of the resurrection of the dead is not confined to

Jew and Greek; it is the heritage of every man of every time and clime; and I am here a demonstrator of the power of man."

16. Then He arose and pressed the hand of every man and of the royal host, and said:

17. "Behold, I am not myth made of the fleeting winds, for I am flesh and bone and brawn, but I can cross the borderland at will."

18. And they talked together there a long, long time. Then Jesus said:

19. I go my way, but you shall go to all the world and teach the gospel of the omnipotence of man, the power of truth, the resurrection of the dead."

20. "He who believes this gospel of the son of man shall never die; the dead shall live again."

21. Then Jesus disappeared, but He had sown the seed. The words of life were spoken in Orissa, and all of India heard.

22. The Magician priests were in the silence of Persepolis, and Kasper and the Magician masters, who were first to greet the child of promise in the shepherd's home in Bethlehem, were with the priests.

23. And Jesus came and sat with them; a crown of light was on His head.

24. And when the silence ended Kasper said, "A master from the Royal Council of the Silent Brotherhood is here; let us give praise.

25. And all the priests and masters stood and said, "All hail! What message from the Royal Council do you bring?"

26. And Jesus said, "My brothers of the Silent Brotherhood, peace on earth, good will to men."

27. The problem of the age has been solved; a son of man has risen from the dead; has shown that human flesh can be transformed into flesh divine.

28. Before the eyes of men this flesh in which I come to you was changed with speed of light from human flesh. And so I am the message that I bring to you.

29. To you I come, the first of all the race to be transmuted to the image of Allah.

30. What I have done, all men will do; and what I am, all men shall be.

31. But Jesus said no more. In one short breath He told the story of His mission to the sons of men, and then He disappeared.

32. The Magi said, "Some time ago we read this promise, now fulfilled, upon the dial plate of heaven."

33. And then we saw this man who has just demonstrated unto us the power of man to raise from carnal flesh and blood to flesh of Allah, a babe in Bethlehem.

34. And after many years He came and sat with us in these same groves.

35. "He told the story of His human life, of trials, sore temptation, buffeting and woes.

36. He pressed along the thorny way of life till He has risen and overthrown the strongest foes of Allah and man; and He is now the only master of the human race whose flesh has been transmuted into flesh divine.

37. He is the God-man of to-day, but every one of earth shall overcome and be like Him, a Son of Allah.

These events occurred before he was thirty years of age, and the events after He had risen from the dead, He appeared back to India, Europe and Africa in the land of Egypt, and made Himself known unto the world. These events are the eighteen years which are absent in your "Holy Bible."

The Events of John the Baptist.

John taught by the Egyptian sage.

The meaning of Baptism and how to baptize himself.

And after He was baptized, He was taken at the age of twelve years into Africa, the land of Egypt, and there remained in the Egyptian Schools 18 years.

And there he learned his duty as "Fore-runner of Jesus."

CHAPTER XX.

HOLY INSTRUCTION AND WARNINGS FOR ALL YOUNG MEN

1. Beware, young men, beware of all the allurements of wantonness, and let not the harlot tempt thee to excess in her delights.

2. The madness of desire shall defeat its own pursuits; from the blindness of its rage, thou shalt rush upon destruction.

3. Therefore give not up thy heart to her sweet enticements, neither suffer thy soul to be enslaved by her enchanting delusions.

4. The foundation of health which must supply the stream of pleasure, shall quickly be dried up, and every spring of joy shall be exhausted.

5. In the prime of thy life old age shall overtake thee; the sun shall decline in the morning of thy days.

6. But when virtue and modesty enlighten her charms, the lustre of a beautiful woman is brighter than the stars of heaven, and the influence of her power it is in vain to resist.

7. The whiteness of her bosom transcendeth the lily; her smile is more delicious than a garden of roses.

8. The innocence of her eyes is like that of the turtle; simplicity and truth dwell in her heart.

9. The kisses of her mouth are sweeter than honey; the perfumes of Arabia breathe from her lips.

10. Shut not thy bosom to the tenderness of love; the purity of its flame shall ennoble thy heart, and soften it to receive the fairest impressions.

CHAPTER XXI

MARRIAGE INSTRUCTIONS FOR MAN AND WIFE FROM THE NOBLE PROPHET

1. Give ear, fair daughter of love, to the instructions of prudence and let the precepts of truth sink deep in thy heart; so shall the charms of thy mind add lustre to the elegance of thy form; and thy beauty, like the rose it resembleth, shall retain its sweetness when its bloom is withered.

2. In the spring of thy youth, in the morning of thy days, when the eyes of men gaze on thee with delight, and nature whispereth in thine ear the meaning of their looks; ah, hear with caution their seducing words; guard well thy heart, nor listen to their soft persuasions.

3. Remember thou art made man's reasonable companion, not the slave of his passion: the end of thy being is not merely to gratify his loose desire, but to assist him in the toils of life, too soothe his heart with thy tenderness, and recompense his care with soft endearments.

4. Who is she that winneth the heart of man, that subdueth him to love, and reigneth in his breast?

5. Lo! Yonder she walketh in maiden sweetness, with innocence in her mind, and modesty on her cheek.

6. Her hand seeketh employment, her foot delighteth not in gadding abroad.

7. She is clothed with neatness, she is fed with temperance; humility and meekness are as a crown of glory circling her head.

8. On her tongue dwelleth music, the sweetness of honey floweth from her lips. Decency is in all her words, in her answers are mildness and truth.

9. Submission and obedience are the lessons of her life, and peace and happiness are her reward.

10. Before her steps walketh prudence, and virtue attendeth at her right hand.

11. Her eye speaketh softness and love ,but discretion with a sceptre sitting on her brow.

12. The tongue of her licentious is dumb in her presence; the awe of her virtue keepeth him silent.

13. When scandal is busy, and the fame of her neighbors is tossed from tongue to tongue; if charity and good nature open not her mouth, the finger of silence resteth on her lip.

14. Her breast is the mansion of goodness, and therefore she suspecteth no evil of others.

15. Happy were the man that should make her his wife; happy the child that should call her mother.

16. She presideth in the house, and there is peace; she commandeth with judgment, and is obeyed.

17. She ariseth in the morning, she considers her affairs, and appointeth to every one their proper business.

18. The care of her family is her whole delight; to that alone she applieth her study; and elegence with frugality is seen in her mansion.

19. The prudence of her management is an hour to her husband, he heareth her praise with a secret delight.

20. She informeth the minds of her children with wisdom; she fashioned their manners from the examples of her own goodness.

21. The words of her mouth is the law of their youth; the motion of her eye commandeth their obedience.

22. She speaketh, and the servants fly; she pointeth, and the thing is done: for the law of love is in their hearts, and her kindness addeth wings to their feet.

23. In prosperity she is not puffed up; in adversity she healed the wounds of fortune with patience.

24. The troubles of her husband are alleviated by her councils and sweetened by her endearments: he putteth his heart in her bosom, and receiveth comfort.

25. Happy is the man that has made her his wife; happy the child that call her mother.

CHAPTER XXII

DUTY OF A HUSBAND

1. Take unto thyself a wife, and obey the ordinance of Allah; take unto thyself a wife, and become a faithful member of society.

2. But examine with care, and fix not suddenly. On thy present choice depends thy future happiness.

3. If much of her time is destroyed in dress and adornment; if she is enamoured with her own beauty, and delighted with her own praise; if she laugheth much, and talketh loud; if her foot abideth not in her father's house, and her eyes with boldness rove on the faces of men: though her beauty were as the sun in the firmament of heaven, turn thy face from her charms, turn thy feet from her paths, and suffer not thy soul to be ensnared by the allurements of imagination.

4. But when thou findest sensibility of heart, joined with softness of manners; and accomplished mind, with a form agreeable to thy fancy; take her home to thy house; she is worthy to be thy friend, thy companion in life, the wife of thy bosom.

5. O cherish her as a blessing sent to thee from heaven. Let the kindness of thy behaviour endear thee to her heart.

6. She is the mistress of thy house; treat her therefore with respect, that thy servants may obey her.

7. Oppose not her inclination without cause; she is the partner of thy cares, make her also the companion of thy pleasures.

8. Reprove her faults with gentleness, exact not her obedience with rigour.

9. Trust thy secrets in her breast; her counsels are sincere, thou shalt not be deceived.

10. Be faithful to her bed; for she is mother of thy children.

11. When pain and sickness assault her, let thy tenderness soothe her affliction: and look from thee of pity and love shall alleviate her grief, or instigate her pain, and be of more avail than ten physicians.

12. Consider the tenderness of her sex, the delicacy of her frame; and be not severe to her weakness, but remember thine own imperfections.

CHAPTER XXIII

HOLY INSTRUCTIONS FOR THY CHILDREN

1. Consider, thou art a parent, the importance of thy trust; the being thou hast produced, it is thy duty to support.

2. Upon thee also it dependeth whether the child of thy bosom be a blessing or a curse to thyself; an useful or a worthless member, to the

community.

3. Prepare him early with instruction, and season his mind with the maxims of truth.

4. Watch the bent of his inclinations, set him right in his youth and let no evil habit gain strength with his years.

5. So shall he rise like a cedar on the mountains; his head shall be seen above the trees of the forest.

6. A wicked son is a reproach to his father; but he that doth right is an honor to his grey hairs.

7. The soil is thine own, let it not want cultivation; the seed which thou sowest, that also shalt thou reap.

8. Teach him obedience, and he shall bless thee; teach him modesty, and he shall not be ashamed.

9. Teach him gratitude, and he shall receive benefits; teach him charity, and he shall gain love.

10. Teach him temperance, and he shall have health; teach him prudence, and fortune shall attend him.

11. Teach him justice, and he shall be honored by the world; teach him sincerity, and his own heart shall not reproach him.

12. Teach him diligence, and his wealth shall increase; teach him benevolence, and his mind shall be exalted.

13. Teach him science, and his life shall be useful; teach him religion, and his death shall be happy.

CHAPTER XXIV

THE OBEDIENCE OF CHILDREN TOWARDS THEIR FATHER

1. From the secrets of Allah let man learn wisdom, and apply to himself the instruction they give.

2. Go to the desert, my son; observe the young stork of the wilderness; let him speak to thy heart; he beareth on his wings his aged sire; he lodgeth him in safety, and supplieth him with food.

3. The piety of a child is sweeter than the incense of Persia offering to the sun; yea, more delicious than odors wafted from a field of Arabian spices of the western gales.

4. Be grateful to thy father, for he gave thee life and to thy mother, for she sustained thee.

5. Hear the words of his mouth, for they are spoken for thy good; give ear to his admonition, for it proceedeth from love.

6. He hath watched for thy welfare, he hath toiled for thy ease; do honor therefore to his age, and let not his grey hairs be treated with irreverence.

7. Forget not thy helpless infancy, nor the fordwardness of thy youth, and indulge the infirmities of thy aged parents; assist and support them in the decline of life.

8. So shall their hoary heads do down to the grave in peace; and thine own children, in reverence of thy example, shall repay thy piety with filial love.

CHAPTER XXV

A HOLY COVENANT OF THE ASIATIC NATION

1. Ye are the children of one father, provided for by his care; and the breast of one mother hath given you suck.

2. Let the bonds of affection, therefore, unite thee with thy brothers, that peace and happiness may dwell in thy father's house.

3. And when ye separate in the world, remember the relation that bindeth you to love and unity; and prefer not a stranger before thy own blood.

4. If thy brother is in adversity, assist him; if thy sister is in trouble, forsake her not.

5. So shall the fortunes of thy father contribute to the support of his whole race; and his care be continued to you all, in your love to each other.

CHAPTER XXVI

HOLY INSTRUCTIONS OF UNITY

1. The gifts of the understanding are the treasures of Allah; and he appointed to every one his portion, in what measure seemeth good unto himself.

2. Hath he endowed thee with wisdom?

Hath he enlightened thy mind with the knowledge of truth? Communicate it to the ignorant, for their instruction; communicate it to the wise, for thine own improvement.

3. True wisdom is less presuming than folly. These wise men doubteth often, and changeth his mind; the fool is obstinate, and doubteth not; he knoweth all things, but his own ignorance.

4. The pride of emptiness is an abomination; and to talk much, is the foolishness of folly; nevertheless, it is the part of wisdom to hear with patience their impertinence, and to pity their absurdity.

5. Yet be not puffed up in thine own conceit, neither boast of superior understanding; the clearest human knowledge is but blindness and folly.

6. The wise men feeleth his imperfections, and is humbled; he laboreth in vain for his own approbation but the fool peepeth in the shadow stream of his own mind, and is pleased with the pebbles which he seeth at the bottom he bringeth them up, and showeth them as pearls and with the applause of his brethren delighteth himself.

7. He boasteth of attainments in things that are of no worth; but where it is a shame to be ignorant, there he hath no understanding.

8. Even in the path of wisdom, he toileth after folly; and shame and disappointment are the reward of his labor.

9. But the wise man cultivates his mind with knowledge; the improvements of arts is his delight, and their utility to the public crowneth with honor.

Nevertheless, the attainment of virtue he accounteth as the highest learning; and the science of happiness is the study of his life.

CHAPTER XXVII

THE HOLY UNITY OF THE RICH AND THE POOR

1. The man to whom Allah hath given riches, and blessed with a mind to employ them aright, is peculiarly favored and highly distinguished.

2. He looketh on his wealth with pleasure, because it affordeth him the means to do good.

3. He protecteth the poor that are injured; he suffereth not the mighty to oppress the weak.

4. He seeks out objects of compassion; he injureth into their wants; he relieveth them with judgments and without ostentation.

5. He assisteth and rewardeth merit; he encourageth ingenuity and liberally promoteth every useful design.

6. He carrieth his own great works; his country is enriched, and the labor is employed: he formeth new schemes, and the arts receive improvement.

7. He considers the superfluities of his table, as belonging to the poor of his neighborhood; and he defraudeth them not.

8. The benevolence of his mind is not checked by his fortune; he rejoiceth therefore in riches, and his joy is blameless.

9. But woe unto him that heapeth up wealth in abundance, and rejoiceth alone in the possession thereof; that grindeth the face of the poor, and considereth not the sweat of their brows!

10. He driveth on oppression, without feeling; the ruin of brother disturbeth him not.

11. The tears of the orphan he drinketh as milk; the cries of the widow are music to his ears.

12. His heart hardened with the love of wealth; no grief or distress can make impression upon it.

13. But the curse of iniquity pursueth him; he liveth in continual fear; the anxiety of his mind and the rapacious desires of his own soul take vengeance upon him for the calamities he had brought upon others.

14. Oh! What are the miseries of poverty, in comparison with the gnawings of this man's heart!

15. Let the poor man comfort himself, yes, rejoice; for he hath many reasons.

16. He sitteth down to his morsel in peace; his table is not crowded with flatterers and devourers.

17. He is not embarrassed with a train of dependents, nor teased with the clamours of solicitations.

18. Debarred from the dainties of the rich, he escapeth also their diseases.

19. The bread that he eateth, is not so sweet to his taste? The water he drinketh, is not so pleasant to his thirst? Yea, far more delicious water than the richest draughts of the luxurious.

20. His labor preserveth his health, and procureth him a repose, to which the downy bed of sloth is a stranger.

21. He limiteth his desires with humility, and the calm of contentment is sweeter to his soul than all the acquirements of wealth and grandeur.

22. Let not the rich, therefore, presume on his riches; nor the poor in his poverty yield to despondence; for the province of Allah dispenseth happiness to them both.

CHAPTER XXVIII

HOLY INSTRUCTIONS FROM THE PROPHET
MASTER AND SERVANT

1. Repine not, O man, at the state of servitude: it is the appointment of Allah, and hath many advantages; it removeth thee from cares and solicitudes in life.

2. The honor of a servant is his fidelity; his highest virtues are submission and obedience.

3. Be patient, therefore, under the reproofs of thy master; and when he rebuketh thee, answer not again. The silence of thy resignation shall not be forgotten.

4. Be studious of his interests, be diligent in his affairs, and faithful to the trust which he reposeth in thee.

5. Thy time and thy labor belong unto him. Defraud him not thereof, for he payeth thee for them.

6. And thou who are a master, be just to thy servant if thou expecteth from him fidelity; and reasonable in thy commands if thou expecteth ready obedience.

7. The spirit of a man is in him; severity and rigour may create fear, but can never command love.

8. Mix kindness with reproof, and reason with authority; so shall thy admonitions take place in his heart, and his duty shall become his pleasure.

9. He shall serve thee faithfully from the motive of gratitude; he shall obey thee cheerfully from the principle of love; and fail thou not, in return, to give his diligence and fidelity their proper reward.

CHAPTER XXIX

MAGISTRATE AND SUBJECT

1. O thou, the favorite of Heaven, whom the son of men, thy equals, have agreed to raise to sovereign power and set as a ruler over themselves; consider the ends and importance of their trust, far more than the dignity and height of thy station.

2. Thou art clothed in purple, and seated on a throne; the crown of majesty investeth thy temples, the sceptre of power is placed in thy hand; but not for thyself were these ensigns given; not meant for thine own, but the good of thy kingdom.

3. The glory of a king is the welfare of his people; his power and dominion rest on the hearts of his subjects.

4. The mind of a great prince is exalteth with the grandeur of his situation; he revolveth high things, and searcheth for business worthy of his power.

5. He calleth together the wise men of his kingdom; he consulteth among them with freedom, and heareth the opinions of them all.

6. He looketh among his people with discernment; he discovereth the abilities of men, and employeth them according to their merits.

7. His magistrates are just, his ministers are wise, and the favorite of his bosom deceiveth him not.

8. He smileth on the arts, and they flourish; the sciences improve beneath the culture of his hand.

9. With the learned and ingenious he delighteth himself: he kindleth in their breasts emulation; and the glory of his kingdom is exalted by their labors.

10. The spirit of the merchant who extendeth his commerce, the skill of the farmer who enricheth his lands, the ingenuity of the artists the improvements of the scholar; all these he honoreth with his favor, or rewardeth with his bounty.

11. He planteth new colonies, he buildeth strong ships, he openeth rivers for convenience, he formeth harbors for safety, his people abound in riches, and the strength of his kingdom increaseth.

12. He frameth his statues with equity and wisdom; his subjects enjoy the fruits of their labor in security; and their happiness consists in the observance of the law.

13. He foundeth his judgments on the principles of mercy; but in the punishment of offenders, he is strict and impartial.

14. His ears are open to the complaints of his subjects; he restraineth the hands of their oppressors, and he delivereth them from their tyranny.

15. His people, therefore, look up to him as a father, with reverence and love; they consider him as the guardian of all they enjoy.

16. Their affection unto him begetteth in his breast a love of the public: the security of their happiness is the object of his care.

17. No murmers against him arise in their hearts; the machinations of his enemies endanger not the state.

18. His subjects are faithful, and firm in his cause; they stand in his defense, as a wall of brass: the army of a tyrant flieth before them, as chaff before the wind.

19. Security and peace bless the dwelling of his people; and glory and strength encircle his throne forever.

CHAPTER XXX
HOLY INSTRUCTIONS FROM THE PROPHET
THE SOCIAL DUTIES

1. When thou considerest thy wants, when thou beholdest thy imperfections, acknowledge his goodness, O son of humanity, who honored thee with humanity, endued thee with speech, and placed thee in society, to receive and confer reciprocal helps and mutual obligations, Protection from the injuries, thy enjoyments of the comforts and the pleasure of life; all these thou owest to the assistance of others, and couldest not enjoy but in the bands of society.

3. It is thy duty, therefore, to be a friend to mankind, as it is thy interest that man should be friendly to thee.

4. As he rose breatheth sweetness from his own nature, so the heart of a benevolent man produceth good works.

5. He enjoyeth the ease and tranquility of his own breast, and rejoiceth in the happiness and prosperity of his neighbor.

6. He openeth not his ear unto slander; the faults and the failings of men give a pain to his heart.

7. His desire is to do good, and he researcheth out the occasions thereof; in removing the oppression of another, he relieveth himself.

8. From the largeness of his mind, he comprehendeth in his wishes the hapupiness of all men; and from the generosity of his heart, he endeavoreth to promote it.

CHAPTER XXXI

HOLY INSTRUCTION FROM THE PROPHET
JUSTICE

1. The peace of society dependeth on justice; the happiness of individuals, on the safe enjoyment of all their possessions.

2. Keep the desires of thy heart, therefore, within the bounds of moderation; let the hand of justice lead them aright.

3. Cast not an evil eye on the goods of thy neighbor; let whatever is his property be sacred from thy touch.

4. Let no temptation allure thee, nor any provocation excite thee to lift up thy hand to the hazard of his life.

5. Defame him not in his character; bear no false witness against him.

6. Corrupt not his servant to creat or forsake him; and the wife of his bosom, O tempt not to sin.

7. It will be a grief to his heart, which thou canst not relieve; an injury to his life, which no reparation can atone.

8. In thy dealings with men, be impartial and just; and do unto the mas thou wouldest they should do unto thee.

9. Be faithful to thy trust, and deceive not the man who relieth upon thee; be assured, it is less evil in the sight of Allah to steal than to betray.

10. Oppress not the poor, and defraud not his hire the laboring man.

11. When thou sellest for gain, hear the whispering of conscience, and be satisfied with moderation; nor from the ignorance of thy buyer make any advantage.

12. Pay the debts which thou owest; for he who gave thee credit, relieth upon thine honor; and to withhold from him his due, is both mean and unjust.

13. Finally, O son of society, examine thy heart, call rememberence to thy aid; and if in any of these things thou hast transgressed, and make a speedy reparation, to the utmost of thy power.

CHAPTER XXXII

HOLY INSTRUCTIONS FROM THE PROPHET
CHARITY

1. Happy is the man who hath sown in his breast the seeds of benevolence: the produce thereof shall be charity and love.

2. From the fountain of his heart shall rise rivers of goodness; and the streams shall overflow, for the benefit of mankind.

3. He assisteth the poor in their trouble; he rejoiceth in furthering the prosperity of all men.

4. He censureth not his neighbor; he believeth not the tales of envy and malevolence: neither repeateth he their slanders.

5. He forgiveth the injuries of men, he wipeth them from his rememberance; revenge and malice have no place in his heart.

6. For evil he returneth not evil, he hateth not even his enemies, but requiteth their injustice with a friendly admonition,

7. The griefs and anxieties of men excite his compassion; he endeavoreth to alleviate the weight of their misfortunes, and the pleasure of success rewardeth his labor.

8. He calmeth the fury, he healeth the quarrels of angry men, and preventeth the mischiefs of strife and animosity.

9. He promoteth in his neighborhood peace and good will, and his name is repeated with praise and benedictions.

CHAPTER XXXIII

HOLY INSTRUCTIONS FROM THE PROPHET
GRATITUDE

1. As the branches of a tree return their sap to the root, from whence it arose; as a river poureth its streams to the sea, whence the spring was supplied; so the heart of a grateful man delighteth in returning a benefit received.

2. He acknowledgeth his obligation with cheerfulness, he looketh on his benefactor with love and esteem.

3. And if to return it be not in his power, he nourisheth the memory of it in his breast with kindness; he forgetteth it not all the days of his life.

4. The hand of the dangerous man is like the clouds of heaven which drops upon the earth, fruits, herbage and flowers; but the heart of the ungrateful is like a desert of sand which swalloweth with greediness the showers that fall, and burieth them in its bosom, and produceth nothing.

5. Envy not .thy benefactor, neither strive to conceal the benefit he hath conferred; for though to oblige is better than to be obliged, though the act of generosity commandeth admiration, yet the humility toucheth the heart, and is amiable on the sight both of Allah and man.

6. But receive not a favor from the hand of the proud; to the selfish and avaricious have no obligation; the vanity of pride shall expose thee shame; the greediness of avarice shall never be satisfied.

CHAPTER XXXIV

HOLY INSTRUCTIONS FROM THE PROPHET
SINCERITY

1. O thou who are enamoured with the beauty of Truth, and hast fixed thy heart on the simplicity of her charms, hold fast thy fidelity unto her, and forsake her not; the constancy of thy virtue shall crown thee with honor.

2. The tongue of the sincere is rooted in heart; hypocrisy and deceit have no place in his words.

3. He blusheth at falsehood, and is founded; but in speaking the truth, he hath a steady eye.

4. He supporteth, as a man, the dignity of his character; to the arts of hypocrisy; he scorneth to stoop.

5. He is consistent with himself; he is never embarrassed; he hath courage enough for truth; but to lie he is afraid.

6. He is far above the meanness of dissimulation; the words of his mouth are the thoughts of his heart.

7. Yet, with prudence and caution he openeth his lips; he studieth what is right, and speaketh with discretion.

8. He adviseth with friendship; he reproveth with freedom; and whatsoever he promiseth, shall be performed.

9. But the heart of the hypocrite is hid in his breast; he maketh his words in the semblance of truth, while the business of his life is only to deceive.

10. He laugheth in sorrow, he weepeth in joy; and the words of his mouth have no interpretation.

11. He worketh in the dark as a mole, and fancieth he is safe; but he blundereth unto light, and is betrayed and exposed, with dirt on his head.

12. He passeth his days in perpetual constraint; his tongue and heart are forever at varience.

13. He laboreth for the character of a righteous man; and huggeth himself in the thoughts of his cunning.

14. O fool, fool! The pains which thou takest to hide what thou are, are more than would make thee what thou wouldest seem; and the children of Wisdom shall mock at thy cunning, when in the midst of security, thy disguise is stripped off, and the finger of derision shall point thee to scorn.

CHAPTER XXXV

HOLY INSTRUCTIONS FROM THE PROPHET
RELIGION

1. There is but one Allah, the author, the creator, the governor of the world; almighty, eternal, and incomprehensible.

2. The sun is not Allah, though his noblest image. He enlighteneth the world with his brightness; his warmth giveth life to the products of the earth. Admire him as the creature, the instrument of Allah, but worship him not.

3. To the one who is supreme, most wise and beneficient, and to Him alone, belong worship, adoration, thanksgiving and praise:

4. Who hath stretched forth the heavens with his hands, who hath described with his finger the courses of the stars.

5. Who setteth bounds to the ocean, that it cannot pass; and saith unto the stormy winds, "Be still."

6. Who shaketh the earth, and the nations tremble; who dareth his lightnings, and the wicked are dismayed.

7. Who calleth forth worlds by the words of his mouth; who smiteth with his arm, and they sink into nothing.

8. O reverence the majesty of the Omnipotent; and tempt not his anger, lest thou be destroyed.

9. The province of Allah is ever all his works; he ruleth and directeth with infinite wisdom.

10. He hath instituted laws for the government of the world; he hath wonderfully varied them in all beings; and each, by his nature conformeth his will.

11. In the depth of his mind, he revolveth all knowledge; the secrets of futurity lie open before him.

12. The thoughts of thy heart are naked to his view; he knoweth thy determination before they are made.

13. With respect to his prescience, there is nothing contingent; with respect to his providence, there is nothing accidental.

14. Wonderful he is in all his ways; his counsels are inscrutable; the manner of his knowledge transcendeth thy conception.

15. Pay therefore to his wisdom, all honor and veneration; and bow down thyself in humble and submissive obedience to his supreme discretion.

16. The Father is gracious and beneficient; he hath created the world in mercy and love.

17. His creatures of his hand declare his goodness, and their enjoyments speak of his praise; he clothed them with beauty, he supporteth them with food, he preserveth them with pleasure, from generation to generation.

18. If we lift up our eyes to the heavens, his glory shineth forth; if we cast them down on the earth, it is full of his goodness; the hills and the valleys rejoice and sing; fields, rivers and woods resound his praise.

19. But thee, he hath distinguished with peculiar favor; and exalted they station above all creatures.

20. He hath endued thee with reason, to maintain thy dominion; he hath fitted thee with language, to improve by society; and exalted thy mind with the powers of mediation, to contemplate and adore his inimitable perfections.

21. And in the laws he hath ordained as the rule of life, so kindly hath he united thy duty to thy nature that obedience to his precepts is happiness to thyself.

22. O praise his goodness with sons of thanksgiving, and meditate in silence on the wonders of his love: let thy heart overflow with gratitude and acknowledgment, let the language of thy lips speak praise and adoration, let the actions of thy life show thy love to his law.

23. Allah is just and righteous, and will judge the earth with equity and truth.

24. Hath he established his laws in goodness and mercy, and shall he not punish the transgressors thereof?

25. O think not, bold men, because thy punishment is delayed, that the arm of Allah is weakened; neither flatter thyself with hopes that he winketh at thy doings.

26. His eye pierceth the secrets of every heart, and he remembereth them forever; he respecteth not the persons or the stations of men.

27. The high and the low, the rich and the poor, the wise and the ignorant, when the soul hath shaken off the cumberous sackles of this mortal life, shall equally receive, from the sentence of just and everlasting retribution, according to their works.

28. Then shall the wicked tremble and be afraid; but the heart of the righteous shall rejoice in his judgments.

29. O fear Allah, therefore, all the days of thy life, and walk in the paths which he hath opened before thee. Let prudence admonish thee, let temperance restrain, let justice guide thy hand, benevolence

warm thy heart, and gratitude to Heaven inspire thee 'with devotion. These shall give thee happiness in thy present state, and bring thee to the mansions of eternal felicity in the paradise of Allah.

30.   This is the true economy of Human Life.

CHAPTER XXXVI

HOLY INSTRUCTIONS FROM THE PROPHET
KNOW THYSELF

1.   Weak and ignorant as thou art, O man, humble as thou oughtest to be, O child of the dust, wouldest thou raise thy thoughts to infinite wisdom? Wouldest thou see omnipotence displayed before thee? Contemplate thine frame.

2.   Fearfully and wonderfully art thou made; praise therefore thy Creator with awe, and rejoice before him with reverence.

3.   Wherefore of all creatures art thou only erect, but that thou shouldest behold his works? Wherefore art thou to behold, but that thou mayest admire them? Wherefore to admire thou mayest adore their and thy Creator?

4.   Wherefore is consciousness reposed on thee alone, and whence is it derived to thee?

5.   It is not in flesh to think; it is not in bones to reason. The lion knoweth not that worms shall eat him; the ox perceiveth not that he is fed for slaughter.

6.   Something is added to thee, unlike to what thou seest; something informs thy clay, higher than all is the object of thy senses. Behold, what is it?

7.   The body remaineth perfect after it is fled; therefore, it is no part of it; it is immaterial, therefore, it is eternal; it is free to act, therefore it is accountable for its actions.

8.   Knoweth the ass the use of food, because his teeth mow down the herbage? or standeth the crocodile erect, although his backbone is as straight as thine?

9.   Allah formed thee as he formed these; after them all wert thou created; superiority and command were given thee over all, and in his own breath did he communicate to thee the principle of knowledge.

10. . Know thyself and the pride of his creation, the lime uniting divinity and matter; behold a part of Allah himself within thee; remember thine own dignity, nor dare descend to evil or to meanness.

11.   Who planted terror in the tail of the serpent? Who clothed the neck of the horse with thunder? Even he who hath instructed thee to crush the one under thy feet, and to tame the other to thy purpose.

CHAPTER XXXVII

HOLY INSTRUCTIONS FROM THE PROPHET
THE BREATH OF HEAVEN

1.   Vaunt not thy body; because it was first formed; nor of thy brain, because therein thy soul resideth. Is not the master of the house more honorable than its walls

2. The ground must be prepared before corn be planted; the potter must build his furnace before he can make his porcelain.

3. As the breath of heaven sayeth unto the waters of the deep, "This way shall thy billows, roll, and no other; Thus high, and no higher shall they raise their fury;" so let thy spirit, O man, actuate and direct thy flesh; so let it repress its wilderness.

5. Thy body is as the globe of the earth; thy bones the pillars that sustain it on its basis.

6. As the ocean giveth rise to springs, whose waters return again into its bosom through the rivers; so runneth thy life from thy outwards, and so runneth it into its place again.

7. Do not both retain their course forever? Behold, the same Allah ordained them.

8. Is not thy nose the channel to perfumes, thy mouth the path to delicacies?

9. Are not thine eyes the sentials that watch for thee? Yet how often are they unable to distinguish truth from error?

10. Keep thy soul in moderation; teach thy spirit to be attentive to its good; so shall these its ministers be always to thee conveyances of truth.

11. Thine hand is not a miracle? Is there in the creation aught like unto it? Wherefore was it given thee, but that thou mightest stretch it out to the assistance of thy brother?

12. Why of all things living are thou alone made capable of blushing? The world shall read thy shame upon thy face: therefore do nothing shameful.

13. Fear and dismay, who rob thy countenance of its ruddy splendour? Avoid guilt, and thou shalt know that fear is beneath thee; that dismay is unnamely.

14. Wherefore to thee alone speaks shadows in the vision of the pillow? Reverence them; for know, that dreams are from on high?

15. Thou man alone canst speak. Wonder at thy glorious prerogative: and pay to him who gave it thee a rational and welcome praise, teaching thy children wisdom, instructing the offspring of thy loins in piety.

CHAPTER XXXVIII

HOLY INSTRUCTIONS FROM THE PROPHET
THE SOUL OF MAN

1. The blessing, O man of thy external part, are health, vigour and proportion. The greatest of these is health. What health is to the body even that is honesty to the soul.

2. That thou hast a soul is of all knowledge the most certain, of all truths the most plain unto thee. Be meek, be grateful for it. Seek not to know it perfectly. It is inscrutable.

3. Thinking, understanding, reasoning, willing, call not these the soul. They are its actions, but they are not its essence.

4. Raise it not to high, that thou be not dispised. Be not thou like unto those who fall by climbing; neither debase it to the sense of brutes; nor be thou like to the horse and the mule, in whom there is no understanding.

5. Search it by its faculties; know it by its virtues. They are more in number than the hairs of thy head; the stars of heaven are not to be counted with them.

6. Think not with Arabia, that one soul is parted among all men; neither believe thou with the sons of Egypt, that every man hath many; know, that as thy heart, so also thy soul is one.

7. Doth not the sun harden the clay? Doth it not also soften the wax? As it is one son that worketh both even so it is one soul willeth contraries.

8. As the moon restraineth her nature, thou darkness spread itself before her face as a curtain; so the soul remaineth perfect, even in the bosom of a fool.

9. She is immortal; she is unchangeable; she is alike in all. Health calleth her forth to show her lovliness, and application anointeth her with the oil of wisdom.

10. Although she shall live after thee, think not she was born before thee. She was created with thy flesh, and formed with thy brain.

11. Justice could not give her to thee exalted by virtues, nor mercy deliver her to thee deformed by vices. These must be thine, and thou must answer for them.

12. Suppose not death can shield thee from examination; think not corruption can hide thee from inquiry. He who formed thee of thou knowest not what, can he not raise thee from thou knowest not what again?

13. Perceiveth not the cock the hour of midnight? Exalteth he not his voice to tell thee it is morning? Knoweth not the dog the footsteps of his master? Flieth not the wounded goat unto the herb that healeth him? Yet when these die, their spirit returneth to dust: thine alone surviveth.

14. Envy not to these their sense, because quicker than thine own. Learn that the advantage lieth not in possessing good things, but in the knowing to use them.

15. Hadst thou the ear of the stag, or were thine eyes as strong and piercing as the eagles; didst thou equal the hound in smell, or could the ape resign to thee his taste, or could the tortoise her feeling; yet without reason what would they avail thee? Perish not all these like their kindred?

16. Hath any one of them the gift of speech? Can any say unto thee, "Therefore did I do?"

17. The lips of the wise are as the doors of a cabinet; no sooner are they opened but treasurers are poured out before thee.

18. Like unto trees of gold arranged in beds of silver are wise sentences uttered in due season.

19. Canst thou think too greatly of thy soul? Or can too much be said in its praise? It is the image of Him who gave it.

20. Remember thou its dignity forever; forget not how great a talent is committed to thy charge.

21. Whatsoever may do good, may also do harm. Beware that thou direct its course to virtue.

22. Think not that thou canst lose her in a crowd; suppose not that thou canst bury her in thy closet. Action is her delight, and she will not be withheld from it.

23. Her motion is perpetual; her attempts are universal; her agility is not to be suppressed. It is at the uttermost part of the earth? She will have it. It is beyond the regions of the stars? Yet will her eye discover it. Inquiry is her delight. As one who traverseth the burning sands, in search of water, so is the soul that thirsteth after knowledge.

24. Guard her for she is rash; restrain her, for she is irregular; correct her, for she is outrageous: more supple is she than water, more flexible than wax, more yielding than air. Is there aught that can bind her?

25. As a sword in the hand of a mad man, even so is the soul to him who wanted discretion.

26. The end her search is truth; her means to discover it are reason and experience. But are not these weak, uncertain and fallacious? How then shall she attain unto it?

27. General opinion is no proof of truth, for the generality of men are ignorant.

28. Perception of thyself, the knowledge of Him who created thee, the sense of worship those owest unto Him. Are not these plain before thy face? And, behold! What is there more that men needeth to know?

CHAPTER XXXIX

HOLY INSTRUCTIONS FROM THE PROPHET
PINACLE OF WISDOM

1. As the eye of the morning to the lark, as the shade of the evening to the owl, as honey to the bee, or as the carcass to the vulture even such is life unto the heart of man.

2. Though bright, it dazzleth not; though obscure, it displeaseth not; though sweet, it cloyeth not; though corrupt, it forbiddeth not, yet who is he that knoweth its true value?

3. Learn to esteem as it ought; then are thou near the pinnacle of wisdom.

4. Think not, with the fool, that nothing is more valuable; nor believe, with the pretended wise, that thou oughtest to condemn it. Love it not for thyself, but for the good it may be of to others.

5. Gold cannot buy it for thee neither mines of diamonds purchase back the moment thou hast now lost it. Employ the succeeding ones in virtue.

6. Say not that it were best not to have been born; or, if born, that it has been best to die early; neither dare thou to ask of thy Creator, "Where has been the evil, had I not existed?" Good is thy power, the want of good is evil; and if thy question be just, lo, it condemneth thee.

7. Would the fish swallow the bait if he knew the hook were hidden therein? Would the lion enter the toils if he saw they were prepared for him? So neither, were the soul to perish with this clay, neither would a merciful Father have created him: know hence thou shalt live afterwards.

8. As the bird, enclosed in the cage before he seeth it, yet teareth not his flesh against its sides; so neither labor thou vainly to run the state thou art in, but know it is alloted thee, and be content with it.

9. Though its ways are uneven, yet are they not all painful. Accommodate thyself to all; and where there is the least appearance of evil, suspect the greatest danger.

10. When thy bed is straw, thou sleepest in security; but when thou stretch thyself on roses, beware of the thorns.

11. A good death is better than evil life; strive therefore, to live as long as thou oughtest, not as long as thou canst. While thou life is to others worth more than thy death, it is thy duty to preserve it.

12. Complain not, with the fool, of thy shortness of thy time: remember, that with thy days the cares are shortened.

13. Take from the period of thy life the useless part of it, and what remaineth?

14. Take off the time of thine infancy, thy second infancy of age, thy sleep, thy thoughtless hours, thy days of sickness; and, even at thy fulness of years, how few seasons hast thou truly numbered!

15. He who gave thee life as a blessing, shortened it to make it more so.

16. To what end would longer life have served thee? Wishest thou to have had an opportunity of more vices? As to the good, will not He who limited thy span, be satisfied with the fruits of it.

17. To what end, O child of sorrow, wouldest thou live longer? To breathe, to eat, to see the world? All this thou hast done often already. To frequent repetition, is it not tiresome? Or is it not superfluous?

18. Wouldest thou improve thy wisdom and thy virtue? Alas! What are thou to know? Or who is it that shall teach thee? Badly thou employest the little thou hast; dare not, therefore, to complain that the more is not given thee.

19. Repine not at thy want of knowledge; it must perish within the grave. Be honest here, thou shalt be wise hereafter.

20. Say not unto the crow, "Why numberest thou seven times thy lord?" or to the fawn, "Why are thine eyes to see my offspring an hundred generations?" Are these to be compared with thee in the abuse of life?

21 Are they riotous? Are they cruel? Are they ungrateful? Learn from them, rather, that innocence of manners are the paths of good old age.

22. Knowest thou to employ life better than these? Then less of it may suffice thee.

23. Man, who dares enslave the world, when he knows he can enjoy his tyranny but for a moment, what would he not aim at, if he were immortal.

24. Enough hath thou of life, but thou regardest it not; thou art not in want of it, O man, but thou art prodigal; thou threwest it lightly away, as if thou hadst more than enough; and yet thou repinest that it is not gathered again unto thee. Know, that it is not abundant which maketh rich, but Economy.

25. The wise continueth to live from his first period; the fool is always beginning.

26. Labor not after riches first, and think thou wilt afterwards enjoy them. He who neglecteth the present moment, throweth away all that he hath. As the arrow passeth through the heart while the warrior knew not that it was coming; so shall his life be taken away, before he knoweth that he hath it.

27. What then is life, that man should desire it? What, breathing, that he should covet it.

28. Is it not a scene of delusion, a series of misadventures, a pursuit of evils linked on all sides together? In the beginning, it is ignorance, pain is in its middle; and its end is sorrow.

29. As one wave pusheth evil to evil, in the life of man; the greater and the present swallow up the lesser and the past. Our terrors are real evils; our expectations look forward into impossibilities.

30. Fools, to dread as mortals, and to desire as if immortal!

31. What part of life is it that we should wish to remain with us? Is it youth? Can we be in love with outrage, licentiousness, and temerity? Is it age? Then we are found in infirmities.

32. It is said, grey hairs are revered, and length of days in honor. Virtue can add reverence to the bloom of youth; and without it, age plants more wrinkles in the soul than on the forehead.

33. Is age respected because it hateth riot? What justice is in this, when it is not age that despiseth pleasure, but pleasure that despiseth age.

34. Be virtuous while thou are young, so shall thine age be honored.

CHAPTER XL

HOLY INSTRUCTIONS FROM THE PROPHET
THE INSTABILITY OF MAN

1. Inconstancy is powerful in the heart of man; Intemperance swayeth it whither it will; Despair engrosseth much of it; and Fear proclaimeth. "Behold, I sit unrivalled therein," but Vanity is beyond them all.

2. Weep not therefore at the calamities of the human state; rather laugh at its follies. In the hands of the man addicted to vanity. life then is but the shadow of a dream.

3. The hero, the most renowned of human character, what is he, but the bubble of this weakness. The public is unstable and ungrateful. Why should the man of wisdom endanger himself with fools?

4. The man who neglecteth his present concerns, to revolve how he will behave when greater, feedeth himself with wind, while his bread is eaten by another.

5. Act as becometh thee in the present station, and in more exalted ones thy face shall not be ashamed.

6. What blindeth the eye, or what hideth the heart of a man from himself, like Vanity? Lo, when thou seest not thyself, then others discover thee, most plainly.

7. As the tulip, that is gaudy without smell, conspicious without use; so is the man who sitteth himself up so high, and hath not merit.

8. The heart of the vain is troubled while it seemeth content; his cares are greater than his pleasures.

9. His solicitude cannot rest with his bones, the grave is not deep enough to hide it; he extendeth his thoughts beyond his being; he bespeaketh praise, to be paid when he is gone; but whosoever promiseth it, deceiveth him.

10. As the man who engageth his wife to remain in widowhood, that she disturb not his soul; so is he who expecteth that his praise shall reach his ears beneath the earth, or cherish his heart in its shroud.

11. Do well whilst thou livest; but regard not what is said of it. Content thyself with deserving praise, and thy posterity shall rejoice in hearing it.

12. As the butterfly who seeth not his own colors, as the jasmine which feeleth not the scent it casteth around it; so is the man who appeareth gay, and biddeth others to take note of it.

13. "To what purpose," saith he, "Is my vesture of gold, to what end are my tables filled with dainties, if no eye gaze upon them, if the world knew it not?" Give thy raiment to the naked, and thy food unto the hungry; so shalt thou be praised, and feel that thou deserveth it.

14. Why bestoweth thou in every man the flattery of unmeaning words? Thou knowest, when returned thee, thou regardest it not. He knoweth he lieth unto thee, yet he knoweth thou wilt thank him for it. Speak in sincerity, and thou wilt hear with instruction.

15. The vain delighteth to speak of himself; but he seeth not that others like not to hear him.

16. If he hath done anything worth praise, if he possesses that which is worthy of admiration, his joy is to proclaim it, his pride to hear is reported. The desire of such a man defeateth itself. Men say not. "Behold, he hath done it," or "See, he possesseth it," but, "Mark how proud he is of it."

17. The heart of man cannot attend at once to many things. He who fixeth his souls on show, loseth reality. He pursueth bubbles, which break in their flight, while he treads to earth what would him honor.

CHAPTER XLI

HOLY INSTRUCTIONS FROM THE PROPHET
INCONSTANCY

1. Nature urgeth thee to inconstancy, O man! Therefore guard thyself at all times against it.

2. Thou art, from the womb of thy mother, various and wavering, from the loins of the father inheritest thou instability. How then shalt thou be firm?

3. Those who gave thee a body, furnish it with weakness; but he who gave thee a soul, armed thee with resolution. Employ it, and thou art wise, be wise, and thou art happy.

4. Let him who doeth well, beware how he boasteth of it, for rarely is it of his own will.

5. Is not the event of an impulse from without, born of uncertainty, enforced by accident, dependent on some what else? To thee, and to accident, is due the praise.

6. Beware of irresolution in the intent of thy actions; beware of instability in the execution; so shalt thou triumph over two great failings of thy nature.

7. What reproacheth reason more than to act contrarieties? What can suppress the tendencies to these, but firmness of mind.

8. The inconstant feeleth that he changeth, but he knoweth not why; he seeth that he escapeth from himself, but he perceiveth not how. Be thou incapable of change, in that which is right, and men will rely upon thee.

9. Establish unto thyself principles of action, and see that thou ever act according to them.

10. So shall thy passions have no rule over thee; so shall thy constancy ensure unto thee the good thou possesseth, and drive from thy door misfortune. Anxiety and disappointment shall be strangers to thy gates.

11. Suspect not evil in anyone until thou seest it; when thou seest, forget it not.

12. Whoso hath seen an enemy, cannot be a friend; for man mendeth not of his faults.

13. How should his actions be right, who hath no rule of his life? Nothing can be just which proceedeth not from reason.

14. The inconstant hath no peace in his soul; neither can be at ease whom he concerneth himself with.

15. His life is unequal; his motions are irregular; his soul changeth with the weather.

16. To-day he loveth thee, to-morrow thou art detested by him; and why? Himself knoweth not wherefore he now hateth.

17. To-day he is the tyrant, to-morrow thy servant is less humble; and why? He who is arrogant without power, will be servile where there is not subjection.

18. To-day he is profuse, to-morrow he grudgeth unto his mouth that which it should eat. Thus it is with him who knoweth not moderation.

19. Who shall say of the camelion, "He is black," when, the moment after the verdure of the grass, overspreadeth him?

20. Who shall say of the inconstant, "He is joyful," when his next breath shall be spent in sighing?

21. What is the life of such a man, but the phantom of a dream? In the morning he riseth happy, at noon he is on the rack; this hour he is a god, the next below a worm; one moment he laugheth, the next he weepeth; he now willeth, in an instant he willeth not, and in another he knoweth not whether he willeth nor no.

22. Yet neither case nor pain have fixed themselves on him; neither is he waxed greater, or become less; neither hath he had cause for laughter, or reason for his sorrow; therefore shall none of them abide with him.

23. The happiness of the inconstant is as a palace built on the surface of the sand; the blowing of the wind carrieth away its foundation; What wonder then that it falleth?

24. But what exalted form is this, that hitherward directs its even, its uninterrupted course—whose foot is on earth, whose head is above the clouds?

25. On his brow sitteth majesty; steadiness is in his port; and in his heart reigneth tranquility.

26. Though obstacles appear in his way, he deigneth not to look down upon them; though heaven and earth oppose his passage, he proceedeth.

27. The mountains sink beneath his tread; the waters of the ocean are dried up under the sole of his foot.

28. The tiger throweth herself across his way in vain; the spots of the leopard glow against him unregarded.

29. He marcheth through the embattled legions; with his hands he putteth aside the terrors of death.

30. Storms roar against his shoulders, but are not able to shake them; the thunder bursteth over his head in vain; the lightning serveth but to show the glories of his countenance.

31. His name is Resolution! He cometh from the utmost part of the earth he seeth happiness afar off before him; his eye discovereth her temple beyond the limits of the pole.

32. He walketh up to it, he entereth boldly, and he remaineth there forever.

33. Establish thy heart, O man, in that which is right; and then know, the greatest of human is to be immutable.

CHAPTER XLII

HOLY INSTRUCTIONS FROM THE PROPHET
WEAKNESS

1. Vain and inconstant as thou art, O child of imperfection, how canst thou be weak? Is not inconstancy connected with frailty? Can there be vanity without infirmity? Avoid the danger of the one, and thou shalt escape the mischiefs of the other.

2. Wherein art thou most weak? In that wherein thou seemest most strong; in that wherein most thou glories; even in possessing the things which thou hast; in using the good that is about thee.

3. Art not thy desires also frail? Or knowest thou even what it is thou wouldest wish? When thou hast obtained what most thou soughtest after, behold, it contenteth thee not.

4. Wherefore loseth the pleasure that is before thee its relish? And why appeareth that which is yet to come the sweeter? Because thou art wearied with the good of this, because thou knowest not the evil of that which is not with thee. Know that to be content, is to be happy.

5. Couldst thou choose for thyself, would thy Creator lay before thee all that thou could ask for, would happiness then remain with thee, or would joy always dwell in thy gates?

6. Alas! Thy weakness forbiddeth it; thy infirmity declareth against it. Variety is to thee in the place of pleasure; but that which permanently delighteth, must be permanent.

7. When that is gone, thou repentest the loss of it; though, while it was with thee, thou despiseth it.

8. That which succeedeth it, hath no more pleasure to thee; and thou afterwards quarrelest with thyself for preferring it; behold the only circumstance in which thou arrest not!

9. Is there any thing in which thy weakness appeareth more, than in desiring things? It is in the possessing, and in the using of them.

10. Good things cease to be good in our enjoyment of them. What nature meant pure sweets, are sources of bitterness to us, from our delights arise, pain, from our joys, sorrow.

11. Be moderate in the enjoyment, and it shall remain in thy possession; let thy joy be founded on reason, and to its end shall sorrow be a stranger.

12. The delights of love are ushered in by sighs, and they terminate in languishment and dejection. The objects thou burnedst for, nauseates with satiety; and no sooner hast thou possessed it, but thou art weary of its presence.

13. Join esteem to thy admiration, unite friendship with the love; so shalt thou find in the end content so absolute, that it surpasseth raptures, tranquility more worth than ecstacy.

14. Allah hath given thee no good, without its admixture of evil; but he hath given thee also the means of throwing off the evil from it.

15. As joy is not without its alloy, so neither is sorrow without its portion of pleasure. Joy and grief, though unlike, are united. Our own choice can only give them to us entire.

16. Melancholy itself often giveth delight, and the extremity of joys are mingled with tears.

17. The best things in the hands of a fool may be turned to his destruction; and out of the worst, the wise will find means of good.

18. So blonded is weakness in thy nature, O man, that thou hast not strength either to be good nor to be evil, entirely. Rejoice that thou canst not excel in evil, and let the good that is within thy reach content thee.

19. The virtues are alloted to various stations. Seek not after impossibilities, nor grieve that thou canst not possess them all.

20. Wouldst thou at once have the liberality of the rich, and the contentment of the poor? Shall the wife of thy bosom be despised because she showeth not the virtues of the widow?

21. If thy father sink before thee in the divisions of thy country, can at once thy justice destroy him, and thy duty save his life?

22. If thou behold thy brother in the agonies of a slow death, is it not mercy to put a period to his life? And is it not also death to be his murderer?

23. Truth is but one; thy doubts are of thine own raising. He who made virtues what they are, planted in thee a knowledge of their pre-eminence. Act as thy soul dictates to thee, and the end shall be always right.

CHAPTER XLIII

HOLY INSTRUCTIONS FROM THE PROPHET
THE INSUFFICIENCY OF KNOWLEDGE

1. If there is anything lovely, if there is anything desirable, if there is anything within the reach of man that is worthy of praise, is it not knowledge? And yet who is it that attaineth it?

2. The statesman proclaimeth that he hath it; the ruler of the people claimeth the praise of it—but findeth the subject that he possesseth it?

3. Evil is not requisite to man; neither can vice be necessary to be tolerated; yet how many evils are permitted by the connivance of the laws: How many crimes committed by the degrees of the council!

4. But be wise, O ruler, and learn, O thou that are to command the nations! One crime authorized by these is worse than the escape of ten from punishment.

5. When the people are numerous, when thy sons increase about thy table; sendest thou them not out to slay the innocent, and to fall before the sword of him whom they have not offended?

6. If he objects of thy desire demanded the lives of a thousand sayeth thou not? "I will have it." Surely thou forgettest that He who created thee, created also these; and that their blood is as rich as thine.

7. Sayest thou, that justice cannot be executed without wrong? Surely thine own words condemn thee.

8. Thou who flatterest with false hopes the criminal that he may confess his guilt, art not thou unto him a criminal? Or is thy guiltless, because he cannot punish it?

9. When thou commandest to the torture him who is but suspected of ill, darest thou to remember, that you mayest rack the innocent?

10. Is thy purpose answered by the event? Is thy soul satisfied with his confession? Pain will enforce him to say what is not, as easy as what is, and anguish hath caused innocence to accuse herself.

11. That thou mayest not kill him without cause, thou dost worst than kill him; that thou mayest prove if he be guilty, thou destroyeth him innocent.

12. O blindness to all truth! O insufficience of the wisdom of the wise! Know, when thy judge shall bid thee account for this, thou shalt wish ten thousand guilty to have gone free, rather than one innocent then to stand forth against thee.

13. Insufficient as thou art to the maintenance of justice, how shalt thou arrive at the knowledge of truth? How shalt thou ascend to the footstep of her throne?

14. As the owl is blinded by the radiance of the sun, so shall the brightness of her countenance dazzle thee in thy approaches.

15. If thou wouldest mount onto her throne, first bow thyself at her footstool; if thou wouldest arrive at the knowledge of her, first inform thyself of thine own ignorance.

16. More worth is she than pearls, therefore seek her carefully; the emerald, and the sapphire, and the ruby are as dirt beneath her feet; therefore pursue her manfully.

17. The way to her is labor; attention is the pilot that must conduct thee into her port. But weary not in the way; for when art arrived at her, the toil shall be to thee for pleasure.

18. Say not unto thyself, "Behold, truth breedeth hatred, and I will avoid it; dissimulation raiseth friends, and I will follow it." Are not the enemies made by truth, better than the friends obtained by flattery?

19. Naturally doth man desire the truth; yet, when it is before

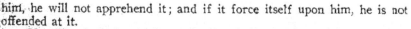

him, he will not apprehend it; and if it force itself upon him, he is not offended at it.

20. The fault is not in truth, for that is amiable; but the weakness of man bareth not its splendour.

21. Wouldst thou see thine insufficience more plainly? View at thy devotions! To what end was religion instituted, but to teach thee thine infirmities, to remind thee of thy weakness, to show thee that from Heaven alone art thou to hope for good?

22. Doth it not remind thee that thou art dust? Doth it not tell thee that thou art ashes? And behold repentence, is not frailty?

23. When thou givest an oath; when thou swearest thou wilt not deceive; behold it spreadeth shame upon thy face, and upon the face of him that receiveth it. Learn to be just, and repentance may be forgotten; learn to be honest, and oaths are unnecessary.

24. The shorter follies are, the better: say not therefore to thyself, "I will not play the fool by halves."

25. He that heareth his own faults with patience, shall reprove another with boldness.

26. He that giveth a denial with reason, shall suffer a repulse with moderation.

27. If thou art suspected, answer with freedom. Whom should suspicion affright, except the guilty?

28. The tender of the heart is turned from his purpose by supplications, the proud is rendered more obstinate by entreaty; the sense of thine insufficience commandeth thee to hear; but to be just, thou must hear without thy passions.

CHAPTER XLIV

HOLY INSTRUCTIONS FROM THE PROPHET
MISERY

1. Feeble and insufficient as thou art, O man, in good; frail and inconstant as thou art in pleasure; yet there is a thing in which thou art strong and unshaken. Its name is Misery.

2. It is the character of thy being, the prerogative of thy nature; in thy breast alone, it resideth; without thee, there is nothing of it. And behold, what is its scource, but thine own passions?

3. He who gave thee these, gave thee also reason to subdue them; exert it, and thou shall trample them under thy feet.

4. Thine entrance into the world, is it not shameful? Thy destruction, is it not glorious?—Lo! men adorn the instruments of death with gold and gems, and wear them above their garments.

5. He who begetteth a man, hideth his face; but he who killeth a thousand, is honored.

6. Know thou, notwithstanding, that in this is error. Custom cannot alter the nature of truth; neither can the opinion of man destroy justice; the glory and the shame are misplaced.

7. There is but one way for a man to be produced: there are a thousand by which he may be destroyed.

8. There is no praise or honor to him who giveth being to another; but triumphs and empire are the rewards of murder.

9. Yet he who hath many children, hath as many blessings; and he who hath taken away the life of another, shall not enjoy his own.

10. While the savage curseth the birth of his son, and blesseth the death of his father, doth he not call himself a monster?

11. The greatest of all human ills is sorrow; to much of this thou are born unto; add not unto it by thine own perverseness.

12. Grief is natural to thee, and is always about thee; pleasure is a stranger, and visiteth thee by times: use well thy reason, and sorrow shall be cast behind thee; be prudent, and the visits of joy shall remain long with thee.

13. Every part of thy frame is capable of sorrow, but few and narrow are the paths that lead to delight.

14. Pleasures can be admitted only simply, but pains rush in a thousand at a time.

15. As the blaze of straw fadeth as soon as it is kindled, so passeth away the brightness of joy, and thou knowest not what become of it.

16. Sorrow is frequent, pleasure is rare: pain cometh of itself: delight must be purchased: grief is unmixed; but joy wanteth not, its alloy of bitterness.

17. As the soundest health is less perceived than the lightest malady, so the highest joy touchest us less deep than the smallest sorrow.

18. We are in love with anguish; we often fly from pleasure: when we purchase it, costeth it not more than it is worth?

19. Reflection is the business of man; a sense of his state is his first duty; but who remembereth himself a boy? Is it not in mercy, then, that sorrow is allotted unto us?

20. Man forseeth the evil that is to come; he remembereth it when it is past; he considereth not that the thought of affliction woundeth deeper than the affliction itself. Think not of thy pain, but when it is upon thee, and thou shalt avoid what most hurt thee.

21. He who weepeth before he needeth, weepeth more than he needeth; and why, but that he loveth weeping?

22. The stag weepeth not till the spear is lifted against him; nor do the tears of the beaver fall, till the hound is ready to seize him: man anticipateth death by the apprehension of it; and the fear is greater misery than the event itself.

23. Be always prepared to give an account of thine actions; and the best death is that which is least premediated.

CHAPTER XLV

THE DIVINE ORIGIN OF THE ASIATIC NATIONS

1. The fallen sons and daughters of the Asiatic Nation of North America need to learn to love instead of hate; and to know of his higher self and lower self. This is the uniting of the Holy Koran of Mecca, for teaching and instructing all Moorish Americans, etc.

2. The key of civilization was and is in the hands of the Asiatic nations. The Moorish, who were the ancient Moabites, and the founders of the Holy City of Mecca.

3. The Egyptians who were the Hamitites, and of a direct descendant of Mizraim, the Arabians, the seed of Hagar, Japanese and Chinese.

4. The Hindoos of India, the descendants of the ancient Canaaites, Hititites and Moabites from the land of Canaan.

5. The Asiatic nations and countries in North, South and Central America; The Moorish Americans and Mexicans in North America. Brazilians, Argentinians and Chilians in South America.

6. Columbians, Nicaraguans and the natives of San Salvador in Central America, Etc. All of these are Moslems.

7. The Turks are the true descendants.of Hagar, who are the chief protectors of the Islamic Creed of Mecca; Beginning from Mohammed the first, the founder of the uniting of Islam, by the command of the great universal God—Allah.

CHAPTER XLVI

THE BEGINNING OF CHRISTIANITY

1. The foundation of Christianity began in Rome. The Roman nations founded the first Church of whom crucified Jesus of Nazareth for seeking to redeem his people from under the Roman yoke and law.

2. Jesus himself was of the true blood of the ancient Canaanites and Moabites and the inhabitants of Africa.

3. Seeking to redeem his people in those days from the pressure of the pale skin nations of Europe, Rome crucified Him according to their law.

4. Then Europe had peace for a long time until Mohammed the first came upon the scene and fulfilled the works of Jesus of Nazareth.

5. The holy teaching of Jesus was to the common people, to redeem them from under the great pressure of the hands of the unjust. That the rulers and the rich would not oppress the poor. Also that the lion and the lamb may lay down together and neither would be harmed when morning came.

6. These teachings were not accepted by the rulers neither the rich; because they loved the principles of the tenth commandments.

7. Through the tenth commandments the rulers and the rich live, while the poor suffer and die.

8. The lamb is the poor people, the lion is the rulers and the rich, and through Love, Truth, Peace, Freedom and Justice all men are one and equal to seek their own destiny; and to worship under their own vine and fig tree. After the principles of the holy and divine laws of their forefathers.

9. All nations of the earth in these modern days are seeking peace, but there is but one true and divine way that peace may be obtained in these days and it is in through Love, Truth, Peace, Freedom and Justice being taught universally to all nations, in all lands.

CHAPTER XLVII

EGYPT, THE CAPITOL EMPIRE OF THE DOMINION OF AFRICA

1. The inhabitants of Africa are the descendants of the ancient Canaanites from the land of Canaan.

2. Old man Cush and his family are the first inhabitants of Africa who came from the land of Canaan.

3. His father Ham and his family was second. Then came the word Ethiopia, which means the demarcation line of the dominion of Amexem, the first true and divine name of Africa. The dividing of the land between the father and the son.

4. The dominion of Cush, North-East and South-East Africa and North-West and South-West was his father's dominion of Africa.

5. In later years many of their brethren from Asia and the Holy lands joined them.

6. The Moabites from the land of Moab who received permission from the Pharaoahs of Egypt to settle and inhabit North-West Africa; they were the founders and are the true possessors of the present Moroccan Empire. With their Canaanite, Hititite and Amorite brethren who sojourned from the land of Canaan seeking new homes.

7. Their dominion and inhabitation extended from Northeast and Southwest Africa, across the great Atlantis even unto the present North South and Central America and also Mexico and the Atlantis Islands. Before the great earthquake, which caused the great Atlantic Ocean.

8. The River Nile was drudged and made by the ancient Pharoahs of Egypt, in order to trade with the surrounding kingdoms. Also the Niger River was drudged by the great Pharoah of Egypt in those ancient days for trade, and it extends eastward from the River Nile, westward across the great Atlantic. It was used for trade and transportation.

9. According to all true and divine records of the human race there is no negro, black, or colored race attached to the human family, because all the inhabitants of Africa were and are of the human race, descendants of the ancient Canaanite nation from the holy land of Canaan.

10. What your ancient forefathers were, you are today without doubt of contradiction.

11. There is no one who is able to change man from the descendant nature of his forefathers; unless his power extends beyond the great universal Creator Allah himself.

12. These holy and divine laws are from the Prophet, Noble Drew Ali, the founder of the uniting of the Moorish Holy Temple of Science of North America.

13. These laws are to be strictly preserved by the members of all the Temples, of the Moorish Holy Temple of Science. That they will learn to open their meetings and guide it according to the principles of Love, Truth, Peace, Freedom and Justice.

14. Every subordinate Temple of the Grand-Major Temple is to form under the covenant of Love, Truth, Peace, Freedom and Justice; and create their own laws and customs, in conjunction with the laws of the Holy Prophet and the Grand Temple. I, the Prophet, Noble Drew Ali, was sent by the great God, Allah to warn all Asiatic of America to repent from their sinful ways; before that great and lawful day which is sure to come.

15. The time has come that every nation must worship under his own vine and fig tree, and every tongue must confess his own.

16. Through sin and disobedience every nation has suffered slavery, due to the fact that they honored not the creed and principles of their forefathers.

17. That is why the nationality of the Moors was taken away from them in 1774 and the word negro, black and colored was given to the Asiatics of America who were Moorish descent, because they honored not the principles of their mother and father, and strayed after the gods of Europe whom they knew nothing of.

THE END OF TIME AND THE FULFILLING OF THE PROPHESIES

1. The last Prophet in these days is Noble Drew Ali, who was prepared divinely in due time by Allah to redeem men from their sinful ways; and to warn them of the great wrath which is sure to come upon the earth.

2. John the Baptist was the forerunner of Jesus in those days, to warn and stir up the nation and prepare them to receive the divine creed which was to be taught by Jesus.

3. In these modern days there came a forerunner, that was divinely prepared by the great God-Allah and his name is Marcus Garvey, who did taught and warn the nations of the earth to prepare to meet the coming Prophet; who was to bring the true and divine Creed of Islam, and his name is Noble Drew Ali: who was prepared and sent to this earth by Allah, to teach the old time religion and the everlasting gospel to the sons of men. That every nation shall and must worship under their own vine and fig tree, and return to their own and be one with their Father God-Allah.

4. The Moorish Holy Temple of Science is a lawfully chartered and incorporated organization. Any subordinate Temple that desire to receive a charter, the prophet has them to issue to every state throughout the United States, Etc.

5. That the world may hear and know the truth, that among the descendants of Africa there is still much wisdom to be learned in these days for the redemption of the sons of men under Love, Truth, Peace, Freedom and Justice.

6. We, as a clean and pure nation descended from the inhabitants of Africa, do not desire to amalgamate or marry into the families of the pale skin nations of Europe. Neither serve the gods of their religion, because our forefathers are the true and divine founders of the first religious Creed, for the redemption and salvation of mankind on earth.

7. Therefore we are returning the Church and Christianity back to the European Nations, as it was prepared by their forefathers for their earthly salvation.

8. While we, the Moorish Americans are returning to Islam, which was founded by our forefathers for our earthly and divine salvation,

9. The covenant of the great God-Allah, "Honor thy father and thy mother that thy days may be longer upon the earth land, which the Lord thy God, Allah hath given thee!"

10. Come all ye Asiatic of America and hear the truth about your nationality and birthrights, because you are not negroes. Learn of your forefathers ancient and divine Creed. That you will learn to love instead of hate.

11. We are trying to uplift fallen humanity. Come and link yourselves with the families of nations. We honor all the true and divine prophets.

The fallen sons and daughters of the Asiatic Nation of North America need to learn to love instead of hate; and to know of his higher self and lower self. This is the uniting of the Holy Koran of Mecca, for the teaching and instructing for all Moorish Americans, etc.

Made in the USA
Monee, IL
02 March 2022

92137820R00042